Folk Belief and
Traditions of the Supernatural

BEEWOLF PRESS

Published in Denmark
by Beewolf Press
an imprint of Island Dynamic
Lyneborggade 21, st. / 2300 København S / Danmark

All papers within this book were subject to double-blind peer review.

Copyright © Island Dynamics and chapter contributors 2016

Cover photo © Adam Grydehøj

ISBN: 978-87-996331-4-2

EDITED BY
TOMMY KUUSELA

&

GIUSEPPE MAIELLO

Folk Belief and
Traditions of the Supernatural

Beewolf

Contents

Preface

Tommy Kuusela
Stockholm University, Sweden

Giuseppe Maiello
Palacký University, Czech Republic

In the spring of 2014, Island Dynamics arranged joint conferences on Unst, Shetland, Britain's northernmost island: *Folk Belief and Traditions of the Supernatural* (25-30 March 2014) and *The Supernatural in Literature and Film* (29-31 March 2014). Both conferences were prepared and organized with unceasing energy and care by Adam Grydehøj (Island Dynamics, Denmark). The first conference, *Folk Belief and Traditions of the Supernatural*, of which the present volume is a direct result, explored past and present supernatural traditions worldwide, focusing on how they relate to experience, place, ritual, and narrative. The conference was a collaboration of the Department of Folklore & Ethnology at Indiana University, the Anthropological Institute at Nanzan University, and the Folklore Society (UK). There was a full programme of lectures and excursions, with many of the former being included in revised form in this volume. Each of the accepted papers has been peer reviewed and subjected to evaluation by two scholars. We hope that these will appear elsewhere in the future. This volume also includes papers that were not part of the conference.

There can be little question about the importance of Shetland, with its exciting history and rich folk life, as the heart for a conference on folk beliefs and the supernatural. In the days preceding the sessions, trips were taken across Shetland's North Isles (Yell, Fetlar, and Unst) and to sites associated with the supernatural and local legends, as well as natural wonders, archaeological sites, and museums. We also had a chance to explore the town of Lerwick and the Shetland Museum & Archives. We met with craftsmen and local tradition bearers. Special thanks are due to our wonderful guides: Elizabeth Morewood, Robert Thomson, Tony Mouat, Alex Nicholson, and Andrew Jennings (who has contributed to this volume with his knowledge of folklore on Fetlar). Two professional storytellers also joined our ranks and shared their tales: Mark Lawson (Whitstable, England) and Anna Fancett (University of Aberdeen, Scotland). The group stayed in cottages at Saxa Vord, close to a small brewery called Valhalla, the most northerly brewery in the United Kingdom. One of its beverages, 'The White Lady', takes its name from a local legend of a ghostly apparition of an old woman who is said to appear in vehicles, usually driven by lone males, on a lonely stretch of road just three miles from the brewery. The legend can of course be recognized as the urban legend motif of a vanishing or ghostly hitchhiker.

The conference call for papers attracted submissions from Asia, Australia, Europe, and North America. The majority of the articles in this volume were presented at the conference and represent the great breadth of approaches being taken on the supernatural from a wide-ranging geographical scope. Sessions were held at North Unst Public Hall, on the island of Unst. The conference sessions, as well as the excursions on the beautiful islands of Shetland, were stimulating and combined love of scholarship with a spirit of friendship and cheer that characterized the conference as a whole. The present volume bears witness to the importance of the supernatural from different academic fields, and it is clear that theories and concepts of what constitutes the supernatural have a wide applicability. Last but not least, we hope that you will enjoy these edited, peer-reviewed proceedings of the *Folk Belief and Traditions of the Supernatural* conference.

Folk Belief and Traditions of the Supernatural

Chapter 1
Some Thoughts on the Supernatural, the Fantastic and the Paranormal in Medieval and Modern Literature

Arngrímur Vídalín
Center for Research in the Humanities, University of Iceland

What does 'supernatural' mean?
We tend to imagine that we know very much what terms such as 'supernatural' mean, and even that we all always understand them exactly as they were intended to be understood. It is all too easy to forget that context may make a world of difference, that 'the supernatural' can be taken to mean different things in different cultures, that different academic disciplines may view it and make use of it with varying emphasis and meaning, and of course that what would now be considered supernatural may not at all be the same as would have been thought of as being supernatural in previous centuries.

To know what is supernatural entails knowing what is not supernatural. What makes a particular being supernatural, and when, by the same token, does a supernatural being cease to be supernatural? Does the origin story of the being matter, if one is given? Dracula is originally a man, albeit bloodthirsty, who is then transformed into a literally bloodthirsty vampire. Is Dracula a supernatural creature, or is he a man with supernatural properties?

Do the supernatural properties he acquires, in other words, become such an integral part of him through his transformation into a vampire that he is made supernatural by them? In the world of the novel *Dracula*, what would it mean to be supernatural?

In Stephen King's *It*, the reader is introduced to a creature that by most people's standards is obviously supernatural: a vicious clown that attacks and brutally murders children and can take any form feared by them. The clown takes on the forms of the Wolfman, a mummy, and the father of Beverly Marsh, one of the main characters, to name a few examples. By the end of the novel, the monster is revealed to be some kind of ancient alien life form. Does it cease to be supernatural at this point, now that it has been revealed to be a force of nature older than humanity? Is the supernatural, in this sense, not something that merely seems to be contrary to nature until an explanation has been found, thus always remaining natural? Such a re-evaluation of the nature of the monster occurs in the 13th Century Icelandic saga *Hrólfs saga Gautrekssonar*, where a troll comes to the court of the Irish king, resulting in the panic and terror of everyone present. It is soon revealed that this troll has a name, Þórir járnskjöldr, and once he has been named, he assumes humanity and ceases to be a troll (cf. Á. Jakobsson 2009a: 192-193). But would a troll be supernatural? In fact, what is a troll? Even that term, as it is used in saga literature, has incredibly many layers of meaning, making trolls virtually impossible to define (Á. Jakobsson 2008: 105-110). I will come back to this point later on.

It seems to me, then, that there are two kinds of definitions of the supernatural making the rounds in academic discourse. The first is an understanding of the supernatural in modern terms, as something which does not belong to the natural world and thus cannot exist in reality (this is not to speak of what Alaric Hall has aptly named the 'social reality' of such phenomena in folk-belief, cf. Hall 2007:9). By this view, one may contend that vampires are supernatural, and that the alien monster of *It* is supernatural to the reader, because it can only exist inside the novel (or so we hope). I have previously used this approach to illustrate that most purportedly supernatural beings in the sagas of the Icelanders most definitely belong to the natural realm (i.e. that which is accepted as being either corporeally or spiritually real) of the saga universe (Vídalín 2012: 55-149). I have since come to realize that this approach is inherently flawed except when it is applied to modern literature, as I was applying an anachronistic understanding of the supernatural onto medieval texts (for an interesting comparison of different types of such 'supernatural' encounters, see Sävborg 2009; see also Vídalín 2013b, in which I compare this sense of the 'supernatural' with the 'fantastic'). The other approach is to restrict ourselves to what 'supernatural' meant at the time of writing of the literature we aim to scrutinize – assuming we can reach a consensus on what that definition of the supernatural would entail. In the Middle Ages, the supernatural meant that which exists beyond nature, the higher powers: God and the divine order, miracles and angels (see e.g. Mitchell 2009: 285-287); demonic phenomena were supernatural as well, as according to Augustinian theology, nothing existed but through the virtue of God (cf. Vídalín 2013a: 181-186). In the dualist worldview of Medieval Catholicism, there could therefore exist two kinds of supernatural phenomena: *miraculosa* and *magica*, i.e. acts of God and the acts of the Devil. Those phenomena that belonged without certainty to either group, those of unexplained origin, were termed *mirabilia* (Tulinius 1999: 291-292).

   Neither approach seems to me to be satisfactory when analyzing what traditionally has been categorized as 'the supernatural'. The first approach is both inexact and anachronistic. To borrow terminology from Hall (2007: 9), it relies too heavily on a modern understanding of objective reality while measuring Medieval social realities. The second approach, however, while accurate from the point of view of the theologian, idea-historian, or the folklorist, leads us in a wholly different direction from the monsters, werewolves, and "other beings from outside the observable natural world" (Mitchell 2009: 285) we are accustomed to think of when speaking of the supernatural. This is what I mean when I say that we all like to think that we know what we are talking about when we use words like 'supernatural', yet at the same time there is no good way of using them so as to make sure our choice of words is accurate and that everyone is on the same page. What the problem seems to come down to is thus a poor choice of words. The question is not as it seemed: what *is* the supernatural, as if that is necessarily what we are looking at, but rather: what *might be* an adequate term with which folklorists, historians, philologists, and literary critics alike might employ to group this mess of assorted phenomena to better understand them?

What might be the function(s) of the supernatural?
As with the supernatural as a general concept we all ironically claim to understand, so we tend to be certain (at least sometimes) that we can evaluate whether an occurrence is of supernatural origin based merely on a cursory reading of its description. It is rare that the question is posed: what, if anything, makes this particular encounter supernatural? And in what sense, if any, is it supernatural?

First, I would like to venture the thought that, through stigma attached to the very notion, we tend to think of the supernatural as something evil or foreboding. It is something negative or contrary to nature that awaits us, lurking out in the wilderness and the darkness, all too eager to tear us to bits in the blink of an eye and carry our carcass to its lair. The supernatural may also be shocking to behold, whether good or ill. It may be an item imbued with magical properties, the act of a sorcerer or a witch, or the very person possessing said magical abilities. The supernatural need not be evil however. As Flint observes (1991: 33; cf. Mitchell 2009: 286), the difference between a good sorcerer and an evil one in the Augustinian view lies in their means and ends rather than the use of magic by itself. The supernatural may be also witnessed in an act of God, such as Jesus walking on a lake or re-animating the dead with positive results, though the dead may sometimes rise of their own accord, and this yields negative results as they wreak havoc upon the living. In Icelandic *afturgöngur* ('re-ambulants'), we may see elements of ghosts, zombies, and vampires all at once in the same creature. It is in the essence of the supernatural that it is something beyond our understanding, though we may sneak glimpses of its truth.

The supernatural is frequently manifested in some sort of challenge awaiting a protagonist to vanquish; had the protagonist not come along, it is implied, the supernatural would have been able to terrorize the innocent longer still. Often in modern works of fiction, the protagonist realizes that she or he is the only hope – such is the case in *It* and such is the case in John Carpenter's 1982 film *The Thing*. But this seems to be a more modern idea. In *Beowulf*, the eponymous hero must defeat the evil Grendel, for no one else seems capable of doing so. Beowulf then kills Grendel's mother and eventually he succumbs to a dragon. While there has been controversy over the nature of the mother (cf. Klaeber 1922; Gilliam 1961; Kuhn 1979; Stanley 1979; Trilling 2007), there is nothing to indicate that either she, her son, nor the dragon are supernatural, though arguably they are monsters (what constituted monstrosity in the Middle Ages is an issue I will deal with separately). The Icelandic counterpart to Beowulf could be said to be Grettir Ásmundarson the Strong, a troll-hunter who, through an encounter with an *afturganga* named Glámr, loses his luck and eventually becomes outlawed from society and is himself likened to trolls, thus becoming the very thing he fought against. Grettir's encounter with a trollwoman at a farm very much resembles Beowulf's mortal fight with Grendel, and the ensuing combat with the trollwoman's male counterpart behind a waterfall is very much akin to Beowulf's fight with Grendel's mother (Jónsson 1946: 212-213, 214-216; Heaney 2000: 140-143, 144-145, respectively). These trolls are absolutely monstrous, not possessing any language as far as anyone knows, living in caves like animals, yet there is nothing in any sense of the word 'supernatural' about them that I can point my finger to, except if I were to passively equate everything monstrous with the supernatural.

The aforementioned battle that Grettir has with Glámr, on the other hand, could be said to have many supernatural elements. Glámr is a shepherd employed by the farmer Þórhallr in Forsæludalr when no one else dares watch over his sheep due to *reimleikar* – which would be directly translatable to 'haunting', although in Old Norse a haunting could either refer to the activity of ghosts or trolls, or both manifested in the same creature as later will be the case with Glámr himself (cf. Á. Jakobsson 2009b: 128-129; Á. Jakobsson 2008: passim). Glámr in his original human form is quite terrifying in appearance, signifying his borderline moral alignment, and he is unafraid of any hauntings or such things so he accepts the job of guarding Þórhallr's sheep almost too brazenly. This could be considered an act of hubris, as he is later found killed at the end of a long trail of destruction. The tracks indicate a great struggle and that the creature fought by Glámr must also have died from its injuries, although it is never found and thus never identified. After his burial at a church, Glámr does not rest. Instead, he so violently haunts Forsæludalr that many inhabitants desert their farms. When he and Grettir meet, they wrestle so fiercely that everything is left broken in their wake, and finally when Grettir defeats him, the clouds move away from the moon so that he can see into Glámr's eyes, the sight of which is the only thing ever to frighten Grettir. At this moment, Glámr puts a curse on him that everything he will accomplish thereafter will be to his own detriment, that he will never reach his full potential in life, that Glámr's eyes will forever follow him in the darkness instilling mortal fear in him, and that he will die in exile. Grettir, regaining his strength, decapitates Glámr and puts his head by his rear (Jónsson 1946: 113-123), a common practice of exorcising ghosts in medieval Iceland (and of dispatching vampires in 18th Century Eastern Europe, cf. Á. Jakobsson 2010; Thorne 1999: 73; a closer comparison between the two may be found in Á. Jakobsson 2009b).

Glámr's curse is later fulfilled down to every detail: Grettir's actions eventually lead to his full outlawry from society, and his fear of the dark is crippling as he dares not dwell on his own in his hiding place on the island Drangey. It is implied that had Grettir not fought with Glámr, he would have reached his physical apex and become virtually indestructible, but that due to the curse his strength remains that of three to four men. But what kind of creature is Glámr, then? Torfi Tulinius offers the explanation for Glámr's re-ambulism that he is a heathen character slowly brought under the power of the Devil, so that he would be *mirabilia* bordering on *magica* (Tulinius 1999: 296). Glámr can thus be considered supernatural in both senses of the word as outlined before, but this is a rather rare occurrence in Old Norse literature except when it comes to those who come back from the dead (cf. Vídalín 2012).

The hero's role in literature remains the same: to prove one's valour in combat. Sometimes in doing so, the hero must fight powerful animals and horrible monsters. In *Brennu-Njáls saga*, the character Þorkell hákr is said, rather matter of factly, to have travelled abroad and killed a *finngálkn* and thereafter a flying dragon, *flugdreki* (Sveinsson 1954: 302-303). What finngálkn means in this context is uncertain, though frequently they are described as a kind of chimera, centaur, or other hybrid creature. That certainly seems strange enough in the mind of the modern reader, but such creatures and other kinds of monsters were without any doubt believed in the Middle Ages to inhabit foreign and especially faraway countries (see e.g. Vídalín 2013a; Friedman 1981; Mittman 2003). The nonchalant way in which Þorkell hákr is said to have disposed of said *finngálkn* and the dragon underlines the fact that the countries in which he encountered them, Finland and Estonia respectively, were considered far enough away from Iceland for it to be plausible that such creatures might inhabit them; in fact, Finland was considered a marginal place in the world by Icelandic and Scandinavian standards, and its inhabitants are frequently described as sorcerers and trolls (Pálsson 1997: 14-27; Vídalín 2013a: 191-204).

Thus it has increasingly become my opinion, the longer I have dealt with the term 'supernatural', that the supernatural does not really lie in the heart of what we are looking for. Unlike modern literature, monsters and the supernatural are rarely interlinked concepts in the Middle Ages. There are countless examples of monsters in historical literature from the advent of writing to modern times. The most influential school of teratology is derived, in part through Heredotus, from Pliny the Elder in his immense 1st Century AD work *Naturalis historia*. Pliny describes various monstrous peoples around the world, such as the headless Blemmyes who have faces in their chests, the Troglodytes who live in caves, the Cynocephali who have the heads of dogs, the Anthropophagi, and many others. These monsters became extremely popular, prompting St. Augustine among others to find a solution to the problem they posed to the Christian worldview. St Augustine's answer was, as briefly touched upon earlier in this article: that monsters, should they exist, must be, as all other creatures, created by God. This became the default explanation in the Middle Ages, re-iterated by St Isidore in his *Etymologiae* in the 7th Century, and propagated from there all over Europe and all the way to Iceland (Vídalín 2013a: 178-191).

Never at any point in history were these monsters considered supernatural as far as I have seen. They have been associated with evil, the armies of the Antichrist, and the apocalypse, but in all the sources I have come across they are always considered to be actual nations of people living in their countries on the margins of the world. Sometimes monstrous births may occur, but I have found no indication of these being considered supernatural either; in fact it seems to have been considered a natural phenomenon that women might give birth to monsters should they experience shock or witness strange things during their pregnancy (cf. Roodenburg 1988; Shildrick 2002: 32-33), and I have found indications of such beliefs in Icelandic sources from the 14th Century, the scientific explanation for which is attributed to Hippocrates himself (Unger 1862: 178-9).

Supernatural or fantastic?
The same principle is in effect when we look at other creatures often associated with the supernatural. Are dragons supernatural? If so, then we must be able to explain how so. Are they supernatural because they cannot exist? Tell that to Medieval audiences of sagas and romances, who very much believed that such creatures could exist. Are they supernatural if they have the ability to speak, and if

so, what is the argument for that particular ability being supernatural when possessed by a dragon? Or do such creatures rather belong to the realm of 'the fantastic'? It is, after all, not uncommon to find the presumption that 'the fantastic' must have something to do with dragons, or otherwise implausible elements of adventures. The problem with 'the fantastic' as a term is that it is even more vague and jejune than 'the supernatural'.

The 2006 Saga Conference in Durham attempted, under the heading 'the fantastic in Old Norse/Icelandic literature', to reach a better understanding of the term and its ramifications for Old Norse literature, and though the two massive volumes of preprints are among the greatest contributions to recent scholarship, the conference left 'the fantastic' just as poorly defined as it had been before, and it has rarely been touched upon since. A few examples of the problem will now follow.

Tatjana Jackson (2006: 426) understands the fantastic as "something created by imagination, not existing in reality" and that the term should therefore be applied "to the introduction of non-realistic details in the sagas that aimed to present the historical past." The 'definition-by-realism' is widely invoked in scholarship, but as far as I can tell that definition is usually based on modern ideas of realism. It is rare to find attempts to grapple with what could seem real in the Middle Ages.

Vésteinn Ólason seems to me to equate 'the fantastic' with fantasy, and in the summary given in Icelandic, it becomes clear that he takes the word 'fantastic' to mean 'strange' (furðulegt) or 'absurd' (fjarstæðukennt) (Ólason 2007: 22) and he uses it almost as a binary opposite to the word 'supernatural'. Ólason shows that he recognizes Todorov, who we will address later, yet for some reason he seems to avoid engaging with his definition of the fantastic (Ólason 2007: 14).

According to Else Mundal (2006: 718), "The fantastic [...] deals with beings and phenomena that do not belong to the real, experienced world, but rather to imagination and fantasy." It seems to me that Mundal delivers 'the fantastic' quite close to the doorstep of *magic realism*, a term most commonly associated with modern literature, but most importantly she argues that 'the fantastic' is something that the audience of a saga would not believe in. Stephen Mitchell (2009: 282) also regards 'the fantastic' as being contrary to the believable, though he makes it explicitly clear when he speaks of 'the fantastic' that it is not a Medieval term, but a modern one. Sometimes 'the fantastic' is evoked without any explanation of its meaning. Sverrir Jakobsson (2006: 940) speaks of giants and dragons belonging to "the realm of the unknown and the fantastic", and Peter Dinzelbacher (2005: 65) speaks of confrontations with "phantastischen Wesen".

These few examples represent a much larger, more diverse arena of 'the fantastic' in scholarship, and, perhaps unsurprisingly, they invariably presume some semantic relation to 'fantasy'. In fact, scholarly discourse is riddled with such vague usage of 'the fantastic' as something to do with fantasy or fairy tales, akin perhaps to Tolkien's speaking dragon Smaug in *The Hobbit*.

A premise for such an idea would have to be that Medieval audiences had a hard time believing in narratives of one sort of strange creature, but that they could very much believe in similar narratives of strange creatures of another sort. Mundal admits that making such a distinction between the believable and unbelievable, and thus between the supernatural and fantastic, is in practicality impossible. As Mitchell rightfully argues, whether audiences found something incredulous, we might never know, and if they did it may or may not have anything to do with what we, the modern readers, find believable. And as we find no indication in particular that medieval audiences considered narratives of supposed 'fantastic' creatures unbelievable, in the sense that we find fantasy literature unbelievable, or in any other sense for that matter, we can hardly presume that 'the fantastic' in this meaning is by any means a term fit to be used in analysis of medieval literature.

In fact, in Medieval texts, we find much indication to the contrary, that at the very least the general possibility of the existence of various creatures – by our modern measure supernatural, fantastic, or what have you – was acknowledged. The fact that we find a flying dragon in *Njáls saga,* considered to belong to the 'realistic' genre of sagas, is not indicative of 'fantastic elements' in an otherwise realistic saga just because we modern readers find such things incredible. In my view, it indicates quite the opposite, that just as in a multitude of sources from the time of Pliny and his monstrous peoples, from St. Augustine's inclusion of said monstrous peoples in Christian doctrine to St. Isidore's popularization of them in a Christian context, from Alexander the Great's letter to Aristotle proclaiming the existence of the Marvels of the East, right down to Sir Mandeville's travels in the 14th Century, that just like these and many other sources indicate: there was a belief in the Middle Ages that strange creatures, peoples, and monsters existed, and yet as we must allow the possibility that many people in the Middle Ages might have been sceptical of the existence of such creatures, they themselves also had to at least allow for the possibility of their existence though they had not seen them with their own eyes.

Which brings me to my second point concerning this: There does indeed exist a proper definition of the term 'the fantastic', and it does apply to Medieval literature in very much a different way from the way it is being used, insofar as we are ready to analyse Medieval literature as fiction (this is in fact the method employed by Chiara Benati 2006). The definition was put forth by Tzvetan

Todorov in his expansive 1970 contribution to literary criticism, *The Fantastic: A Structural Approach to a Literary Genre,* translated into English in 1973. Todorov (1975: 25) defines 'the fantastic' as follows: "The fantastic is that hesitation experienced by a person who knows only the laws of nature, confronting an apparently supernatural event."

It is clear from the outset that Todorov's 'fantastic' is not an antithesis to the supernatural, but a theory of the reception of modern literature; in other words it is meant to convey the reader's response to an event transpiring within a work of fiction, yet seemingly breaking the natural laws of that fictional universe by taking place. These natural laws that are broken can either be those that the reader assumed was at play in the text, or they may have been implied in the text itself. If, for example, an alien warship suddenly appears and blasts open Buckingham Palace in a Victorian era romance novel, the interplay between character and reader creates a moment of uncertainty as to whether the event is really transpiring or not, or in Todorov's words: "The fantastic, we have seen, lasts only as long as a certain hesitation: a hesitation common to reader and character, who must decide whether or not what they perceive derives from "reality" as it exists in the common opinion" (Todorov 1975: 41).

'The fantastic' is thus not the same as magic realism; it is a reactionary effect that can be caused by magic realism or the use of unbelievable elements within a narrative. An author consciously employing techniques akin to magic realism is therefore a prerequisite for 'the fantastic' to ever occur. 'The fantastic' is not the speaking dragon in a Medieval saga; it is not even Tolkien's speaking dragon, and neither of those dragons are shown to be so unbelievable within their respective narratives that they should ever have a fantastic effect upon their respective audiences. Quite to the

[19]

contrary, dragons are even to be expected in Medieval sagas as they many times appear in them, and they are most certainly to be expected in modern fantasy literature.

To summarize these two points and perhaps venture an opinion on where to go from here, we first have the way in which 'the fantastic' is being employed to signify phenomena (or understandings thereof) which are entirely absent from the literature, through the supposition that they are to be found all over the place. This is all a matter of definition, as I have argued, that though the phenomena described as 'fantastic' are indeed widely presented in medieval literature, they indeed are not 'fantastic' in any respect at all. They just are. Some of them may be supernatural, most of them are not, but none of them are fantastic.

Secondly, the uncertainty of how to deal with these phenomena once they occur, whether to believe in them or consider them to be supernatural within the believable world of the narrative at hand, is instead what 'the fantastic' as a concept is meant to describe. But even then we come off short-handed as the fantastic only exists through the interplay of us, the readers, and the protagonist of a narrative as the event occurs within said narrative — while we read it. It is a *Schrödinger's Cat* sort of situation, and until it has been resolved to be either one or the other, supernatural or imaginary, it remains both at once, or in other words: fantastic.

Can we say with any measure of certainty that Medieval narratives possessed such a capability for their intended audiences? No. We cannot be sure. For those of us who accept Todorov's definition of 'the fantastic', it is only possible to speak of the occurrence of the fantastic from the point of view of the modern reader, and unless we are studying the reception of Medieval literature in modern times it is a term we should by all means avoid to invoke. It seems that we are facing a term that in Medieval studies neither means what it is supposed to signify, nor does that signification find place in the literature it is applied to.

The paranormal

Here, I have briefly touched upon some of the problematics of widely accepted terminology. 'The supernatural' is problematic in studies of Medieval literature because either it means forcing modern conceptions of what the supernatural is on societies that mostly did not share our understanding of what it is, but if used correctly it restricts our analysis to the Christian dichotomy between good and evil, divine and demonic, and the interplay between these two greater powers behind and above nature. 'The fantastic' is problematic in studies of Medieval literature because it also forces us either to impose our modern ideas of fantasy or the believable onto societies that most certainly did not share our understanding of the real as opposed to the imagined, societies in which actual belief in imaginary beings was widespread or, on the other hand, if we employ the fantastic as Todorov intended, we are anachronistically analyzing literary motifs and techniques which we have no indication of being consciously in use at the time. Indeed they probably were not.

This means that both terms can be used without trouble in analysis of modern literature, if the way in which they are used is clearly defined. On the other hand, only one of them can be properly used when analyzing Medieval literature, and then only in a very narrow sense. The question then remains how we are to advance our studies of certain phenomena in Medieval literature if we cannot go forward with the supernatural marker. The problems with the supernatural term listed in this discussion, as well as many others, have prompted some scholars to let go of the term in favour of 'the paranormal'.

I stated earlier in this essay that perhaps we have been too focused on trying to understand *the* supernatural in literature, and thus actively forcing this purported supernatural into being where perhaps there was nothing particularly supernatural to be found; that perhaps we should instead seek to understand the phenomena before attaching this label to it, that another term might more adequately describe what it is we are dealing with. 'The paranormal' has been suggested as a solution to this problem. 'The paranormal' may be understood as that which is out of the ordinary, that which threatens the boundary of the explicable, that which lies outside of normal experience. The paranormal does not imply a belief or lack of belief in the phenomena it is used to describe; it does not impose on the subject a cultural or anachronistic layer of meaning, even though it is a modern term and is a very self-conscious one at that. Thus dragons are paranormal, regardless of their characteristics, trolls and ghosts are paranormal, and so are magic, miracles, and demonic activity. Monsters are paranormal because they are not frequently encountered. Instead of arguing over modern notions of demarcation such as the rather meaningless supernatural/fantastic dichotomy, it is both possible and feasible instead to seek understanding of paranormal encounters in historical or legendary texts.

That is not to say that the term 'supernatural' might not sometimes be exactly the right term for certain encounters or phenomena, for sometimes the paranormal is also supernatural, but it does release from our shoulders a burden of a discourse of floating meaning that has not really led us very far. It also releases the Medievalist from the stigma following superstitious-sounding words like 'supernatural' which do not seem to have any relevance for the modern world, whereas the paranormal offers us a link between science and folklore that seems, at least to me, to offer a less biased opportunity of viewing the unexplained, for while the 'supernatural' necessarily implies an origin defying natural law, the 'paranormal' does not.

To answer my initial question then, whether Dracula or the monster from *It* are supernatural, or whether trolls and dragons are supernatural, I propose that the answer is greatly dependent on context and how we as researchers, whether our field is literature, folklore, history, or archaeology, choose to understand the term 'supernatural'. Whether these beings are supernatural is complicated, but then again we can perhaps agree that they all are paranormal.

References

Benati, C. 2006. The Fantastic and the Supernatural in the Saga Ósvalds konungs hins helga: Patterns and functions. In: *The Fantastic in Old Norse/Icelandic Literature: Sagas and the British Isles*, vol. 1, J. McKinnell et al. (Eds.). Durham: The Centre for Medieval and Renaissance Studies, pp. 130-139.

Dinzelbacher, P. 2005. Die Mittelalterliche Allegorie der Lebensreise. In: *Monsters, Marvels and Miracles: Imaginary Journeys and Landscapes in the Middle Ages*, L. Søndergaard & R. Th. Hansen (Eds.). Odense: University Press of Southern Denmark, pp. 65-112.

Flint, V. I. J. 1991. *The Rise of Magic in Early Medieval Europe*. Princeton, NJ: Princeton University Press.

Friedman, J. B. [1981] 2000. *The Monstrous Races in Medieval Art and Thought*. Cambridge: Harvard University Press.

Gillam, D. M. 1961. The Use of the Term 'Aeglaeca' in Beowulf at Lines 893 and 2592. *Studia Germanica Gandensia* 3, pp. 145-169.

Hall, A. 2007. *Elves in Anglo-Saxon England: Matters of Belief, Health, Gender and Identity*. Woodbridge: The Boydell Press.

Heaney, S. (Ed.). 2000. *Beowulf: A New Verse Translation*. London: Faber and Faber.

Jackson, T. N. 2006. The Fantastic in the Kings' Sagas. In: *The Fantastic in Old Norse/Icelandic Literature: Sagas and the British Isles*, vol. 1, J. McKinnell et al. (Eds.). Durham: The Centre for Medieval and Renaissance Studies, pp. 426-434.

Jakobsson, Á. 2008. Hvað er tröll? Galdrar, tröll og samfélagsóvinir. In: *Galdramenn: Galdur og samfélag á miðöldum*, T. Tulinius (Ed.). Reykjavík: Háskólaútgáfan.

Jakobsson, Á. 2009a. Identifying the Ogre: The Legendary Saga Giants. In: *Fornaldarsagaerne, myter og virkelighed: studier i de oldislandske fornaldarsögur Norðurlanda*, A. Lassen et al. (Eds.). Copenhagen: Museum Tusculanums forlag, pp. 181-200.

Jakobsson, Á. [2009b] 2013. The Fearless Vampire Killers: A Note about the Icelandic Draugr and Demonic Contamination in Grettis saga. In: Á. Jakobsson (Author) *Nine Saga Studies: The Critical Interpretation of the Icelandic Sagas*. Reykjavík: University of Iceland Press, pp. 125-137.

Jakobsson, Á. 2010. Íslenskir draugar frá landnámi til lúterstrúar: Inngangur að draugafræðum. In: *Skírnir* 184, pp. 187-210.

Jakobsson, S. 2006. On the Road to Paradise: "Austrvegr" in the Icelandic Imagination. In: *The Fantastic in Old Norse/Icelandic Literature: Sagas and the British Isles*, vol. 2, J. McKinnell et al. (Eds.). Durham: The Centre for Medieval and Renaissance Studies, pp. 935-943.

Jónsson, G. (Ed.). 1946. Grettis saga. In: *Íslenzk fornrit*, 7. Reykjavík: Hið íslenzka fornritafélag.

Klaeber, Fr. (Ed.). [1922]1950. *Beowulf and the Fight at Finnsburg*. Third ed. Boston: Heat.

Kuhn, S. 1979. Old English Aglæca-Middle Irish Olach. In: *Linguistic Method: Essays in Honor of Herbert Penzl*, I. Rauch & G. F. Carr (Eds.). New York: Mouton Publishers, pp. 213-230.

Mitchell, S. 2009. The Supernatural and the fornaldarsögur: The Case of Ketils saga hængs. In: *Fornaldarsagaerne, myter og virkelighed*, A. Ney et al. (Eds.). Copenhagen: Museum Tusculanums Forlag, pp. 281-298.

Mittman, A. 2003. The Other Close at Hand: Gerald of Wales and the 'Marvels of the West'. In: *The Monstrous Middle Ages*, A. Bildbauer & R. Mills (Eds.). Toronto: University of Toronto Press, pp. 97-112.

Mundal, E. 2006. The Treatment of the Supernatural and the Fantastic in Different Saga Genres. In: *The Fantastic in Old Norse/Icelandic Literature: Sagas and the British Isles*, vol. 2, J. McKinnell et al. (Eds.). Durham: The Centre for Medieval and Renaissance Studies, pp. 718-726.

Ólason, V. 2007. The Fantastic Element in Fourteenth Century Íslendingasögur: A Survey. In: *Gripla* 18, pp. 7-22.

Pálsson, H. 1997. *Úr landnorðri: Samar og ystu rætur íslenskrar menningar*. Reykjavík: Bókmenntafræðistofnun Háskóla Íslands.

Roodenburg, H. 1988. The Maternal Imagination. The Fears of Pregnant Women in Seventeenth-Century Holland. In: *Journal of Social History* 21 (4), pp. 701–716.

Sävborg, D. 2009. Avstånd, gräns och förundran. Möten med de övernaturliga i islänningasagan. In: *Greppaminni: Rit til heiðurs Vésteini Ólasyni sjötugum*. M. Eggertsdóttir et al. (Eds.). Reykjavík: Hið íslenska bókmenntafélag, pp. 323-349.

Shildrick, M. 2002. *Embodying the Monster: Encounters with the Vulnerable Self*. California: Sage.

Stanley, E. G. 1979. Two Old English Poetic Phrases Insufficiently Understood for Literary Criticism: Þing Gehegan and Senoþ

Gehegan. In: *Old English Poetry: Essays on Style*, D.G. Calder (Ed.). Berkeley: University of California Press, pp. 67-90.

Sveinsson, E. Ól. (Ed.). 1954. Brennu-Njáls saga. In: *Íslenzk fornrit*, 12. Reykjavík: Hið íslenzka fornritafélag.

Thorne, T. [1999] 2000. *Children of the Night: Of Vampires and Vampirism*. London: Indigo.

Todorov, T. [1973] 1975. *The Fantastic: A Structural Approach to a Literary Genre*. R. Howard (Transl.). Ithaca: Cornell University Press.

Trilling, R. R. 2007. Beyond Abjection: The Problem with Grendel's Mother Again. *Parergon* 24 (1), pp. 1-20.

Tulinius, T. 1999. Framliðnir feður: um forneskju og frásagnarlist í Eyrbyggju, Eglu og Grettlu. In: *Heiðin minni: greinar um fornar bókmenntir*, H. Bessason & B. Hafstað (Eds.). Reykjavík: Heimskringla, pp. 283-316.

Unger, C. R. (Ed.). 1862. *Stjórn: Gammelnorsk bibelhistorie fra verdens skabelse til det babyloniske fangeskab*. Christiania: Feilberg & Landmarks forlag.

Vídalín, A. 2012. *The Supernatural in Íslendingasögur: A Theoretical Approach to Definition and Analysis*. Reykjavík: Tower Press.

Vídalín, A. 2013a. 'Er þat illt, at þú vilt elska tröll þat.' Hið sögulega samhengi jöðrunar í Hrafnistumannasögum. In: *Gripla* 24, pp. 173-210.

Vídalín, A. 2013b. Að mæla róteindir með gráðuboga: Um fantasíuhugtakið í miðaldabókmenntum. In: *Skírnir* 187, pp. 356-380.

Chapter 2

Memories and Metamorphoses: A Short Introduction to the Supernatural Tales and Beliefs from Fetlar in Shetland

Andrew Jennings
University of the Highlands & Islands, Scotland

This short paper will introduce scholars, storytellers, and others interested in the stories of Shetland, particularly the supernatural tales, to the rich trove of material collected by several generations of folklorists from the beautiful island of Fetlar.

Fetlar lies on the eastern side of Shetland, a mere 48 hours' sailing time from the Norwegian coast. The island covers 39 km^2, which is about half the size of Guernsey, and is thus the fourth-largest island in the Shetland archipelago.

The tales from this island comprise the most comprehensive and arguably the most representative collection of stories which make up Shetland's rich storytelling tradition. As anyone who has visited Fetlar will affirm, this is ironic as, at the present time, the island has suffered severe depopulation and is now one of Shetland's least inhabited places. There are only 48 inhabitants, a stark contrast to 1841 when the census recorded a healthy 761. There are more stories than there are people. According to local tradition, this state of affairs was prophesied in the 19th Century by a now-unidentified elderly woman, who predicted that, "There will be a mansion on the Ripples, soldiers on Vord Hill, a harbour in Papil Water, and nothing but a shepherd and his dog" (Grydehøj 2008). In some ways, Fetlar is a Shetlandic version of the remote St Kilda or An Blascaod Mór (Great Blasket Island) in Ireland, an important cultural landscape almost devoid of people.

Fetlar has long had a reputation as a place with a rich folklore heritage. The Faroese scholar Jakob Jakobsen, who visited Shetland at the end of the 19ʰh Century on a mission to research Norse cultural survivals in the dialect and folklore, was surprised that so much information had survived on Fetlar (Laurenson 1964: 51). Another great Scandinavian scholar with a deep and abiding interest in Shetland, the Swede Bo Almqvist, said of Fetlar, that it was "the richest in legendary tradition of the Shetland Islands" (Almqvist 1991: 86). From the 1950s onwards, Fetlar was almost a place of pilgrimage for the scholars of the School of Scottish Studies. Calum MacLean, Peter R. Cooke, Tadaaki Miyake, and Alan Bruford, who made use of his Fetlar material in his excellent study of Shetlandic fairies (Bruford 1997), all found representative recordings of Shetlandic material on the island. Many of their Fetlar recordings can now be accessed online. The *Tobar an Dualchais/Kist o Riches* collaborative project saw thousands of hours of recordings made freely available online.

The extraordinary storytellers interviewed included Jeemsie Laurenson and Catherine Mary Anderson. Jeemsie was born in Aith, Fetlar in 1899, and he lived there as a registrar, writer, fisherman, and crofter. Jeemsie was a legend in his own lifetime and many stories, some true, others apocryphal, were told about him (Shaw & Bruford 1975). Catherine was born on the island in 1886 and spent her life crofting there. The famous storyteller Brucie Henderson, from Arisdale on the nearby island of Yell, who was born in 1891, also provided material.

Some of the stories referred to in this paper are in the form of summaries originally attached to the recordings, which can be accessed by those seeking to hear them told in their original form. Where possible, I have categorised the stories according to the various systems available to folklorists, although these can at times obfuscate rather than clarify. These include the Aarne-Thompson-Uther classification system of folktales (ATU), Stith Thompson's *Motif-Index of Folk-Literature* (letters A to Z), Reidar Christensen's classification of migratory legends (ML), and Alan Bruford's classification of Scottish fairy legends (originally F, which can cause confusion with the motif-index so will here be FA).

Unlike the Faroe Islands, where Jakob Jakobsen collected a corpus of old legendary material (Jakobsen 1898-1901), in Shetland this has been almost completely lost. This difference can be put down to the fact that, whereas the Faroese language survived, Shetland underwent a complete linguistic change associated with the loss of Norn in the 18ᵗʰ Century. However, despite this, Fetlar uniquely has two stories which can be with some confidence regarded as authentic survivals of Norse legendary material.

The first story is associated with the settlement of the township of Funzie, pronounced Finny, on the east coast. Funzie is in origin a Norse place-name, meaning 'the place to head for' or 'the found place' (Jennings 2007). This story seems to be Shetland's only surviving *landnám* 'land taking' story, a genre of such great importance in Medieval Iceland. According to the 18ᵗʰ Century *Old Statistical Account*, there is "a place on the eastmost angle of the island called Funzie, which signifies the place first found out" (Gordon 1791-1799: 549). This tradition was repeated by Samuel Hibbert in his extremely important early 19ᵗʰ Century study of Shetland (Hibbert 1822: 170). The native Shetland scholar Laurence Williamson of Mid Yell in his notes recorded from a source called D.W. the following tradition still current in his time in the late 19th Century:

The first Danish vessel that came to Shetland cast a spell overboard at the bow and noticed it passing to the stern…They came to Funzie but did not find it commodist and went round to Strand to the Nort Wick, that is at Grutin, and landed there and called it Groin. Thence they peopled first Strand and Grutin and Funzie and used up all the peat ground (Johnson 1971: 143).

The second legendary tale concerns a certain Jan Teit. Jakob Jakobsen (1897: 4-7) collected this version from an old fisherman called Thomas Tait, who he describes as "a man of most vivid power of narrative, and the last who could tell the remarkable old story of 'Jan Tait and the Bear'":

The king of Norway sent his chamberlain across to Shetland to collect the 'skat' (tax) due to the crown. The chamberlain came to Fetlar, where the skat was collected at Urie ('Øri') To Urie the udallers came with the 'teinds' or tithes they had to pay. They brought with them their 'bismers'. These bismers were, if I may be allowed the bull, ancient wooden steel-yards. The chamberlain of course had his own bismer, which was considered the standard weight, and on which he tested the udallers' bismers. An udaller by the name of Jan Tait, while paying his butter teind, was accused by the chamberlain of having a false bismer. This at once led to a quarrel, in which Tait denounced the chamberlain's bismer as false, and being threatened by the chamberlain, Jan finally raised his bismer and struck the king's representative dead on the spot. This was, of course, a great crime, for which he was summoned to appear before the king in Norway. Arrived there, Jan went in before the king bare-headed and bare-footed, and carrying an axe in his hand. Jan was a strongly-built man, and had big knobs on

[30]

the joints of his feet. So the king stared at his feet, until Jan suddenly asked him why he was staring so fixedly. The king said that he had never seen such strange feet before. Jan said that if they gave him any offence, he would soon cure that, whereupon he took the axe and hewed off one of the knobs. The king said, that he did not at all wonder that Jan had killed his chamberlain, since he had so little regard for his own flesh and blood. But seeing his courage he would give him one chance to save his life. There was a bear infesting a certain place, and constantly endangering the lives if the inhabitants. If he could catch it and bring it alive before the king, he should be pardoned. Tait then went to an old woman who lived near a spot the bear used to frequent, and asked her all about its ways and habits. She said to him: 'By butter you have got into the present trouble, and by butter you shall get out of it'. Then she advised him to take a kit-full of butter and place it in an open spot in the forest, where the bear used to come, watch there till the bear appeared on the scene and licked the butter, and then, when it had lain down to sleep, seize his opportunity and bind it in ropes. Tait acted according to her advice. The bear, after having licked the butter, felt heavy, lay down and fell asleep, whereupon Tait, who had been watching, hastened to tie the animal with strong ropes. He managed to bring the bear alive before the king, but the king, wanting to get rid of him, ordered him out of his sight, bidding him to take the bear home with him to Shetland. Tait went back to Fetlar with the bear and transported it from there to the island of Yelli-Linga (off the Yell coast), where there is a spot still called 'the Bear's Bait', which name is known by very few people now. There is a green circle in the island said to have been made by the bear's walking around the pole to which it was tethered.

This story includes the motifs: F551.4 Remarkably ugly feet and F628.1.3 Strong man overpowers a bear. Bo Almqvist (1991: 82-113) devotes some time to this tale in his fascinating study of 'The Uglier Foot' stories. He draws our attention to its similarity to the genre of Old Icelandic short stories called *þættir*, and also to specific traits shared with particular tales, such as slaying the king's representative, which occurs in *Rauðúlfs þáttr* (Faulkes 1966: 78-79), and adventurous encounters with wild beasts, such as the story of Auðunn and the polar bear in *Auðunar þáttr vestfirzka* (Christiansen R.T. 1922). There is a particular similarity between Jan Teit and the story told by Snorri Sturluson about þórarinn Nefjólfsson, in *Ólafs saga helga* (Johnsen & Helgason 1930-1941) who also had ugly feet. He had a run in with the irascible King Olaf. However, unlike Jan who had to deal with a bear, þórarinn had to defeat king Hroerekr Dagsson of Hedmark, who he then had to take back to Iceland. The stories are so alike that they surely must have a common origin.

As one would expect of a traditional farming and fishing society, which, when it still existed on Fetlar, was exceptionally poor and insecure by modern standards, belief in magic and in a menacing, supernatural world was strong. Shetland as a whole was a late refuge for such beliefs. Indeed, there is anecdotal evidence that belief in the malign, magical power of witchcraft continued well into the 20th Century (Marwick 1975: 51-52). Jakobsen recorded the word *granderi*, an old Shetland word for witchcraft, from Fetlar (Jakobsen 1928: 259). This word clearly had evil connotations. In Old Norse *að granda* meant to 'hurt or damage' (Cleasby and Vigfusson 1874). He also recorded the verb *to grand* 'to hurt by magic' from the same root (Jakobsen 1928: 259). A number of words in Shetland dialect owe their origin to the practice of witchcraft in the Norse speaking period. For example, Jakobsen also recorded the verb *to galder* 'to speak in a loud foolish manner', which comes from ON *galdra* 'to practice witchcraft'. According to the Icelandic laws, anyone practicing *galdra* could be punished with lesser outlawry (Mitchell 2011: 67)

The survival of many supernatural tales is evidence for the strength of belief. There are tales about dangerous spiritual beings which inhabited both land and sea, and tales about that other half of the magical moiety, witches, always threatening life and fertility. There are also tales about the dead, or perhaps more correctly, the undead.

In the stories, the most frequently used names for the smaller land-based supernatural beings are trow, from the Norse word *troll*, or fairy or even Pict, the pre-Norse inhabitants of the Northern Isles, given a euhemerized afterlife (Grydehøj 2009). There is also evidence for the larger species of supernatural being. H. Williamson related a story about a giant and his wife who dragged an island from Yell Sound to Fetlar, with the intention of building a harbour at the Wick of Gruting. However, pieces kept breaking off, creating many of the stacks around the coast (Williamson H. 1957: 54-55). There seems to be a similarity here with the Faroese tale of the Icelandic giant and his wife who unsuccessfully attempted to drag the Faroe Islands to Iceland. They were turned to stone and remain as stacks off Eiðskollur (Kvideland & Sehmsdorf 1988: 312-313). Jakobsen (1928: 281) lists the name of another Fetlar stack as *de stakk o' Gørasten*, the stack of the Gør's stone. Gør comes from Old Norse *gýgr* a giantess or hag.

In the sea, supernatural beings are associated with seals, called selkies in the Scots language, or, intriguingly, Finns. The use of the word Finn for a supernatural being only occurs in Orkney and Shetland and is a further example of the continuity of Nordic tradition.

Let us look at land beings. There are versions of the migratory tale ML6070 'Fairies send a message', where a fairy receives a message that its child has had an accident. This is Laurence

Williamson's 19th Century version, which is localised at the croft of Taft in Funzie (Finyi):

A Fetlar lad was riding one night on a red mare with a grey foal, from the West Isle to Taft in Finyi. Some say that he was going a sweethearting, some that he had been at Urie with fish. When he went by Stakaberg, he heard a voice saying

Trira rara gonga
Du at rides da red (Thou that ridest the red)
An rens da gre (And runnest the grey)
Tell du Tüna Tivla (Tell thou Tüna Tivla)
At Füna Fivla (That Füna Fivla)
'Es fain e da feyr (Has fallen in the fire)
An brunt her. (And burned her).

When he came into Taft the gyüdman's daughters were going into the byre to 'meat da kye'. One carried the straw and the other one a lamp. The lad repeated the words that he heard. A 'trow' was milking the cows in the byre, and when she heard them, flung her copper pan and fled screaming 'Keir and dül, dat's my bairn at Stakaberg'. People say the pan is still in the house, some say built into the wall and the family never afterwards lacked milk (Williamson L. 1957: 4-5).

Williamson also heard a version from one of his sources where the second character fell into the water instead of the fire, "tell Tüna Tivla, at Nüna Nevla, as velina vatyná: is fallen in the water" (Williamson L. 1957: 5). *Vatyná* is Norn and is exactly equivalent to Norwegian *vatnet* 'the water'.

From the perspective of cultural context, it is fascinating that no similar version of this migratory tale has so far been recorded on mainland Scotland. Versions only appear to occur in the Northern Isles. The Fetlar versions, along with 'purer' versions of the verses from Foula, recorded by Jakobsen (1928: xcv-xcvii), contain clear internal linguistic evidence that shows they are survivals of a story from the Norn-speaking era. That it is essentially a Norse story is clear from the fact that some 70 versions have been collected in Norway from west to north (Christiansen R. 1964: 125). There are even Sami versions. Inger Boberg noted in the monograph *Sagnet om den Store Pans Død,* which traces versions of this story back to the Classical period, that the Shetland versions, including those from Fetlar, bore a close resemblance to versions from northern Scandinavia (Boberg 1934: 85-88). Similarities included the variation that the child fell into water and the fact that the fairy received the message in the byre. A copper pan also appeared in a version from Vega in Hålogaland. This hints at a cultural connection between Shetland and Northern Norway, in addition to those recognised connections to Vestlandet, directly over the sea to Shetland's east.

Despite the survival of ML6070, there are not many tales that Shetland shares exclusively with Norway to the exclusion of mainland Scotland. Bruford (1978) listed a greater number of fairy legends shared by Orkney and Shetland with Scotland, but not with Norway. However, the following tale ML5070 (also ATU 476★★ Midwife in the Underworld; F372.1 'Fairies take human midwife to attend fairy woman') is shared by Scotland, Shetland, and Norway, and of course many other places. A wide range of Norwegian variants of this story have been summarised by Christiansen (1958: 91-99) and there is a study of the Irish variants by Mac Carthaigh (1991). The latter concluded that there were two main redactions of this tale. In the first, the midwife is given an ointment which allows her to see the fairies, while in the second the midwife offers her help to a frog or other pregnant animal, which turns out to be the fairy. The tale is popular in Scotland as

MacDonald (1994-1995: 47) lists 12 examples in the recordings from the School of Scottish Studies, including three from Shetland.

The first Fetlar example belongs to the ointment redaction, although there is a twist, in that the midwife can already see the strange beings. The ointment allows her to see a woman long thought dead. The abduction of a woman by the fairies and the woman appearing dead occurs as fairy legend FA51 in Scotland. This version of the tale is from Spence:

There lived in Fraam Gord [in Unst] a woman called Catherine Tammasdaughter, who practised midwifery. One dark, stormy night, as she and her husband were asleep, a messenger from the trows appeared at the bedside. Instead of the goodman getting up and having a say in the matter, he is thrown by a magic spell into the most profound slumber, so that he is quite oblivious to his wife's departure.

Catherine is soon ready, and is conducted to the seashore, where a small boat is in waiting. The night is dark and murky, and the sea is breaking on the shore, but fearlessly she takes her seat in the tiny skiff. With amazing speed they skim the waves, and soon she is landed in the Wick o' Gröten, in the island of Fetlar. Presently she is ushered into a spacious cavern, where a great company of strange beings are gathered together.

The special object of Catherine's visit is soon accomplished, and she is presented with a tiny pig (jar), containing an ointment for anointing the new-born child. While she is performing this delicate operation, she accidentally touches one of her eyes. No sooner does the mysterious ointment touch the eyelid than she beholds a certain woman of her former acquaintance, who had been some time dead. Calling her by name, she exclaims: 'Lass, what wey is du come here?' 'What ee saw du yon wi?' enquires one of the trows. 'Dis een," replies Catherine, pointing to her left eye. Immediately by an elf -shot she is struck blind on the eye that had been thus mysteriously opened to behold the secrets of this enchanted dwelling. (Spence 1899: 149-151).

Another variant of the midwife story is told by Nicolson. Here the midwife is called by the Scot's word *howdie*. There is no mention of ointment:

There was a Trows' hoose on Stakaberg in Fetlar, and one night the peerie folk from this house sent for a howdie, named Baabie Murray, to assist at a birth. When Baabie was leaving for home a female trow escorted her to the door, and told her that she must throw something over the house as she went. The only thing Baabie could find was her keys, and she flung these over the roof as instructed. When she got home, however, her cow was lying dead in the byre, and the keys were found in the animal's inside. After this the Fetlar bairns used to sing:-

'Haste dee, haste dee, Baabie Murray,

Haste dee, an' be ready noo,

Haste dee, haste dee, Baabie Murray,

Da trows ir shot dy only coo.' (Nicolson 1920: 40)

As chthonic agents of misfortune and disease, the trows appear to have caused Baabie Murray to kill her only cow. In Shetland elf-shot, motif D2066, was known as trow-shot. When an animal fell ill under mysterious circumstances and was described as "hurt frae da grund," it was the trows to blame.

Stackaberg, with various spellings, has been mentioned twice so far. This hill turns up in several stories as the home of Fetlar's trows. Despite being a mere 120m high, it would appear to be Fetlar's very own magic mountain. Many of the supernatural tales congregate around it. In Norway, supernatural beings are often associated with mountains (Bø 1987). So it is likely we are seeing another continuing Norse influence here. Indeed, the supposed dead woman seen by Catherine Tammasdaughter was surely an example of someone who had been *bergtatt* 'taken into the mountains'.

Another tale associated with Stackaberg is a version of FA31 'The fairies quit the district for good', told by Jeemsie Laurenson and recorded and printed by Alan Bruford. An old fairy, the last in Fetlar, was discovered in Stackaberg:

> They met a owld Pick [or Trow] in the underground place in Stackaberg, an they axed her where was the rest o them, an she said that […] they hed to clear out o the place wi James Ingram […] They couldn't stand the prayers of James Ingram. They were supposed to go to Faroe…left Shetland and went to Faroe. (Bruford 1978: 226)

James Ingram is a historical figure. He was an influential 19th Century religious leader. John Nicolson has a variant of this story, but he sets it in a knowe or mound near the Burn o' Furse in North Yell (Nicolson 1920: 17). Fetlar and North Yell belong to the same parish. This story is surely related to other stories about notable preachers being insufferable to the devil, such as the story about Bishop Svedberg of Skara in Västra Götaland, Sweden (Hofberg 1890: 117). The other motif in the story is that of the perpetual recession of the fairies. Henderson and Cowan discuss this motif with reference to Shetland (Henderson & Cowan 2001: 24-30). They quote a laird who in 1838 said, "the Methodist preachers are driving away all the trows and bogies and fairies" (Catton 1838: 117).

Stackaberg also features as the focus for Fetlar versions of FA103 'Learning tunes from the fairies'. Laurence Williamson recorded the story that a woman was sitting one day on Stackaberg and heard the sound of music and dancing within and learned the air and could sing it (Johnson 1971: 36). This type of story is more common in Shetland than in any part of Scotland. This is one of the eleven fairy legend types that Bruford suggested were known in Shetland, Orkney, and the Highlands, but were not mentioned by Christiansen (Bruford 1978: 128-129). However, there are similar stories in Scandinavia where a musician learns tunes from supernatural beings, although in this case they are water spirits such as the Norwegian *fossegrim* 'a being who lives behind the waterfall', or the Swedish *näcken, näkk* 'water horse' (cf. Strömbäck 1970). They are given the number ML4090 'Music Taught by Water Sprite'. Perhaps, the fact that this type of story is particularly common in Shetland could be down to lingering Scandinavian preference, even although the stories have no water association.

Probably the most famous fairy fiddle tune Winjadepla, which is still played today, comes from Fetlar. The summarised version of the tale, as told by Jeemsie Laurenson, who was a great advocate of euhemerising the trows as Picts (Bruford 1997: 123), goes as follows:

Gilbert Laurenson took a keshie [basket] of dried corn to Fivla watermill on the east side [of Fetlar]. He also took several hallows [bundles of straw] to sit on and cover himself with while the mill ground the corn. In the middle of the night he heard a company of Picts [trows, little people] saying that they were going to Stakkaberg, which was a great place for them. They came into the mill so that the women could take the nappies off their bairns [children]. The women exclaimed, "Gloy [straw] moves!" and then realised a man was in the straw, but they decided Gilbert was a good man and played him a tune.

The Picts had various stone rings such as Hjaltadance where they would play the fiddle and dance although they had to be careful not to be caught by the sun. Gilbert had a great ear for music and sang over the tune on the way home. The tune was known as 'Old Gibbie's Tune' or 'Winjadepla'.

Winjadepla is a place in Fetlar and according to one tale it could be dangerous. Laurence Williamson noted that an old woman was torn in pieces by spirits there (Johnson 1971: 107). The odd, prehistoric, circular stone settings called *Hjaltadance* by Jeemsie and marked as Haltadance on the OS maps, are the site of a petrifaction legend. Laurence Williamson recorded it like this:

> Hilytadance, or the fiddlers kru, is a circle of grey stones with one in the centre in a plain in Fetlar. There were four and twenty dancing round their fiddler one night when the daylight surprized them and turned them into grey stones (Johnson 1971: 135).

This is a version on ATU 779E★ Stones as Remains of Outrageous Dancers. This tale is often associated with stone circles, particularly in Cornwall it would seem (Varner 2004: 52). However, the fact that it is supernatural beings petrified by being exposed to daylight, rather than misbehaving maidens dancing on the Sabbath, suggests the survival of another Scandinavian influence. F451.3.2.1 Underground spirits turn to stone at sunrise is a common motif in Norway.

Haltadance takes its name from the word *halt* 'crippled or lame'. Shetland trows, like other fairy beings, had physical shortcomings (F254.1 Fairies have physical disabilities). They were supposed to move with a strange gait. Indeed, another name for a trow in Shetland is a henkie, which means 'someone who limps' (Jakobsen 1897: 116). In Norwegian, 'å hinke' means 'to hop'.

These prehistoric stone settings are not the only structures to be associated with supernatural beings on Fetlar. The island also has the *Finniegirt*, recorded as Funzie Girt on OS maps, a Neolithic or Bronze Age dyke which divides the island in half. Jakobsen (1897: 72-73) suggested the name of this ancient dyke commemorated the Finns, as the Sámi were known. They were, even in the 19ᵗʰ Century in Shetland, known to be magic workers. According to Spence (1899: 25-26), "Even in recent times persons who were marked as being particularly lucky, and those who were supposed to be skilled in the Black Art, were spoken of as Norway Finns." Despite Jakobsen's etymology being suspect, the name perhaps being more prosaically linked to the township of Funzie, or just possibly to the Swedish version of migratory tale ML7065 The Name of the Masterbuilder known in Sweden as the Finn-legend (Fossenius 1943), the dyke was clearly associated in people's minds with the supernatural.

The 'guidman' Kolbenstaft in the north-west of Fetlar did not have a sufficiently good dyke around his property to keep away the sheep which broke in continually and destroyed his corn. One night when he went to bed, he expressed the wish that a dyke sufficient to keep off the troublesome animals might be standing in the morning, when he awoke, even if he should give his best cow for it. Next morning, when he went out, he found a splendid new dyke standing where he had wished it, and at the same time his best cow had disappeared from the byre (Jakobsen 1897: 2-3).

This story may be connected to the story told of the Picts in the 11th Century *Historia Norwegiae* 'History of Norway' which survives in a 16th Century copy from Orkney, which claims that:

These islands were first inhabited by the Picts and the Papar. The Picts, who were only a little bigger than pygmies, worked great marvels in city-building each evening and morning, but at noontide they were utterly bereft of their strength and hid for fear in little subterranean dwellings (Phelpstead 2001).

One might disagree with Jakobsen's etymology of Finniegirt, but the Finns do turn up in Fetlar folklore, where they tend to be closely associated with the sea. For example, according to one story a Norway Finn came across from Norway, catching fish as he went. When he approached Fetlar, he noted a particularly good fishing ground. Unfortunately, a storm blew up and the Finn was blown into the Wick of Funzie, where at the last minute he was rescued by an Aith man. The exhausted Finn in thanks told him of the wonderful fishing ground and promised:

> Ye may hae a tired back an' a heavy hand but niver a faerd hert or a tøm [empty] boat. And so it was, "Aiths Deep" became "Aiths Bank" and no life was ever lost going to or coming from this ground (*Shetland Folk Book* 1951: 5).

Again with this story, like the Finniegirt tale, it might be the pronunciation of the name Funzie which suggested a Finn tale.

Another story which connects the Finns with the sea and fishing tells how a Finn in Norway made a bet with a man from Aith that he would not taste or have fresh fish before Yule in his *skio* 'fish drying shed'. The man caught a fish and was about to win his bet when he was nearly killed by a huge wave. This turned out to be the Finn metamorphosed:

> An Aith man went to Norway. He met a Finn while he was there, who made him a wager, that he would neither taste fish nor have fresh fish in his skio 'drying shed' before Yule. The winter that year was so stormy that the Aith man could not go to sea even to catch bait. So it looked as if he was going to lose the wager. However, on Tammas E'en (20th December), the weather broke. As he had no bait, the Fetlar man dyed a rag in blood from his own foot and used that. It proved to be effective, because he caught an olik 'young ling'. However, as he headed back to shore, the sea arose and threatened to swallow the boat. He used oil from a small keg to smooth the surface of the sea. But as he was crossing the 'String o' de Minnie Stack' a terrible wave came rolling behind him. He seized the oil keg and threw it in the face of the wave and thereby managed to make land. On his return to Norway, the Aith man visited the Finn and

reminded him of their wager and the Finn pointed to a deep scar on his brow and his broken teeth and replied:

> 'I'm paid dear eneuch fir dat olik. Doo didna only smore me wi dy oil bit soved me wi dy oli hjulk' (*Shetland Folk Book* 1951: 5-6).

The Finn's connection with the sea and his ability to metamorphose connects these tales to much earlier references. Grydehøj (2009) is surely correct to link them to Norwegian traditions about the Sámi. *Historia Norwegiae* tells a story about how a Finn, *recte* Sámi, sent his spirit out to accomplish a task in the form of a whale (Phelpstead 2001: 7). While in the *Saga of Halfdan Eysteinsson*, Finn, king of the Sámi, also turns himself into a whale (Pálsson & Edwards 1985: 191).

It seems a reasonable hypothesis that it was in the Northern Isles that stories about Finns changing into sea mammals became entangled with legendary material about merpeople, and that this is the origin of the belief that seals could shed their skins and become people. This was a strongly held belief in Shetland and there are many stories. Here is an example from Fetlar told by Catherine Mary Anderson:

> A man was walking round the banks [cliffs] when he came across a girl combing her hair. He saw what he thought was a skin behind her and grabbed it. She asked for it back but instead he took her home and married her. Later on a little boy told her he'd seen a fine-looking thing hidden in a corn scroo [stack] and she took down the scroo and found her skin. As her husband returned home from the fishing in his boat, he saw two seals coming from the shore. He turned to his crew and said, 'This night I'm a widower, for that's my wife that's gone there.'

Bo Almqvist (1990: 5) suggested that the origins of this story lie in western Ireland and Scotland. He proposed that, in an Irish context, it should be called the Man who Married a Mermaid. From the Celtic west, the tale probably spread to Orkney and Shetland and thence to the Nordic world. However, in the Northern Isles the mermaid has become a seal. Perhaps, it was here that the widespread migratory tale ML4080 The Seal Woman first appeared. This story has a very wide distribution in the North Atlantic, occurring in Orkney, Shetland, the Faroes, Iceland, the Hebrides, and the Lofoten Islands of Norway.

Metamorphosis into a seal was not only the preserve of Finns. It was believed that sea mammals could be witches in disguise. Catherine Mary Anderson told a tale about a witch who attempted to attack a fisherman while in the form of a seal:

An old woman called Minnie, who was supposed to be a witch, lived with her daughter and her husband. All the fishermen were in great fear of her and gave her fish, except for one old skipper who thought it was nonsense. One morning he had a row with her. After the lines were set, he told his crew they could sleep while he had a smoke. He saw a large seal heading straight for the boat and smashed the animal with the ricker [a large gaff]. He woke the crew to haul the lines and as they headed in, told them about his row with the old woman.

When they came ashore they met the old woman's daughter. The skipper said he had seen Minnie and asked how she was. She had fallen over the yard dyke and broken her leg. The skipper said it was a pity it wasn't her neck.

This is an example of the motif G275.12 Animal form injured: witch injured. In an actual witchcraft trial from Shetland in 1644, a certain Marion Pardone was accused of, amongst other crimes, taking the shape of porpoise and attacking fishermen in a boat. She was found guilty and executed at Scalloway (Hibbert 1822: 593-602).

It must always be remembered that Fetlar is an island. It was home to fishermen and it is surrounded by the sea, full of horrors, supernatural and otherwise. It is no surprise that the fishermen of Fetlar, whose lives were full of risk and danger, and upon whose success at catching fish the community was dependent, were particularly aware of supernatural threats. Their whole lives were devoted to appeasing the sea's irresistible power. They had a rich vocabulary of sea-words that replaced the taboo land-based words which could not be uttered at sea, and they had practices like spitting into the mouth of the first fish caught, which was intended to increase their luck and secure a successful catch. At the same time, they feared that evil forces intended to do them harm by upturning their boats and drowning them. They were terrified by frightening monsters like the alarming *brigdi* which chased a Fetlar crew in the 1840s (Marwick 1975: 21), and the terrible, three humped creature seen 28 miles east-south-east of Fetlar in June 1882: "It was one hundred and fifty feet long. It had a huge head covered with barnacles as large as herring barrels [and] a prodigious square mouth" (Marwick 1975: 22).

Fishermen were also fearful of local women who might have a grudge against them and turn out to be metamorphosed witches, or witches who could use other means, such as the use of imitative magic to destroy them. There is an example from Fetlar of the story of the Ship-Sinking Witch, which has been given the tale type ML 3036 by Bo Almqvist (Almqvist 1991: 268):

Andrew Gardner, etc, from [...] were at Funzie in a fouraerin [smaller fishing boat] and James Johnson was there and sent home some wooden goods with them. They were wrecked in the mouth going out and all lost. Johnson found some of his goods ashore as he went home. It was said that some witches, Matty Anderson etc, sat in the burn of Urie with a kap muttering spells, till the water was agitated and the cap 'whomled' at the same moment as the boat was being swamped. They had some grudge against Andrew Gardner (Johnson 1971: 151-152).

A *kap* is a wooden bowl. In his discussion of the legend of the ship-sinking witch, Mac Cárthaigh points out that the earliest known version of this idea refers to Pharaoh Nectanebus in the *Pseudo-Callisthenes* written in the 3rd Century (Mac Cárthaigh 1992-1993: 267). He identifies three redactions. The Fetlar story is Redaction A, which occurs in the Hebrides and in Iceland but is particularly well represented in Ireland. Mac Cárthaigh (1992-1993: 282) suggests that the identity of the witch is not generally given in the Irish or Scottish variants, but here the identity is given. The story was known in other parts of Shetland and Samuel Hibbert (1822: 306) gives an excellent version from Dunrossness in the south Mainland.

Jeemsie Laurenson told another interesting variant, or development of the tale, in which the witch works her magic, not primarily to sink the boat, but rather to ensure the fishermen did not catch any fish. The only way to stop the witch blighting the fishermen's efforts was to go and get the help of another old woman who could work stronger magic:

James Miller was an old man in failing health who was dropped from the crew of a sixareen [larger fishing boat]. His wife, Old Meggie Miller, was a witchy woman, and she said that the skipper and crew would lose much more before the season was out. In June, the boat and its ranksman [partner boat] went off and headed for the Fram Haaf south-east of Fetlar. They caught nothing but hoes [dogfish], although the ranksman was deep with fish. After their third hail [haul] the ranksman went ashore and they took over its meed [spot identified from a landmark], but eventually they too headed ashore.

One of the fishermen said that his crülla [sea word for 'wife'] had warned him that Meggie Miller would witch them. The skipper met a friend [relation], who said Meggie Miller had put the caup [wooden bowl] on them and they would be lucky to get through the season alive.

Meggie had a poor amiss [simple-minded] girl to assist her. She sat with her back to the girl and instructed her to agitate the water in a big basin with the caup in it. She got her to haul empty strings from the water and recite: "Tuim [bare, empty], tuim, tuim, tuim."

The skipper had to go to old Meggie o Gru, who had stronger power to break the spell. She promised to help for a bit of fish as long as the minister didn't find out. She gave the skipper some hay from an enchanted knowe [hillock], which he was to tie to the steeds [sinker stones] on the line. This worked, and they were the most successful boat that season. Later the skipper went to the merchant and got him to make up a splendid parcel of provisions for Gru. The merchant just smiled as he'd done the same before.

Of course, it was not just at sea that witches worked their magic. As a traditional subsistence society whose worldview included belief in the theory of limited good (Foster 1965), people were always worried that their neighbour's good fortune was a result of witchcraft, possibly at their expense. The belief that witches could steal the profit from milk or butter was deeply embedded in Shetland. Jeemsie Laurenson told an interesting story about a named person who was briefly involved in this type of witchcraft, but then felt guilty and desisted. Kirsty Ganson received two magic stones which allowed her to steal milk and butter:

The following story is typical of the witchcraft beliefs of the old days. It concerns a devout woman from Colbinstoft in Fetlar,

Christian Ganson, known as Kirstie, who married a Laurenson man from Houbie, one of the survivors of the Diana tragedy. Before she left for the south of the isle, an old woman gave her a yellow butter stone and a white milk stone, which she could use with a ritual or a spell in hard times to get these things. These had been given to the old woman's folk by the Picts or trows. Kirstie was to heat the stone and cool it in water before turning it three times sunwise, then point with tongs in the direction of a good cow while saying, 'Tak aa fae until aa is teen, white milk blaa dee from da been [take all from until all is taken, white milk blow you from the bone].' To block the spell again she was to turn the stones against the sun.

A few years after she had been in Houbie township, and the owner of a very indifferent cow, she decided to try the stones. She cast the spell and started churning milk. She hadn't churned long before she realised the spell was working. A day or two after that, the woman whose butter she had stolen, who had young bairns [children] to feed, announced to the township that she was going to the minister to have the witch laid before the kirk session. She exempted the fine young woman who had moved to the township, who simply wouldn't do such a thing. Next day Kirstie buried the two stones deep in the yard and renounced witchcraft. She told the story to Jeemsie Laurenson's grandmother and swore it was true till her dying day.

From the evidence of the tales, magic seems to have been primarily the preserve of old women. However, there is a surviving tale about a warlock, which contains one of the few references to the Book of Black Arts in Shetland, D1266 – Magic Book. This was yet another story from the extraordinary Jeemsie Laurenson.

The Fetlar warlock John Miller offered to share his book of black arts with a neighbour. He moved to Unst, where he got free lodgings with three single sisters, all of whom he courted. He got them to fight one another and the youngest was the strongest so he married her. They separated and he went to Canada to work as a lumberjack. The Fetlar folk later received a newspaper cutting saying that Miller was dead: he had been hanged by his workmates, who had soon learned of his devilish practices.

E.W. Marwick discussed the Book of the Black Arts stories in Orkney and pointed out the similarity to stories about the *svartebøker* in Norway (Robertson 1991: 362-364). In Orkney the book can only be sold for a smaller price than what one paid for it, or if one is lucky it can be passed to a minister. The pages are black and the writing white. The same motifs occur in Norway, and in a story from Lofoten (Blix 1965: 22,27), the svartbok has black pages and white and red writing. Actual black books, such as Vinjeboka survive in Norway. The occurrence of stories about the Black Book in the Northern Isles can be viewed as yet another connection with the Nordic world.

As well as believing in, and fearing, malevolent supernatural beings and the malign power of witches the people of Fetlar, like other Shetlanders, also had a fear of the dead. Shetlandic children were taken to 'view da dust' to prevent the dead person or 'Thing-at's-awa' haunting the child (Marwick 1975: 94). When speaking of a dead person their name was taboo and circumlocutions had to be used (Marwick 1975: 93). Unbaptised children, the dead who had unfinished business and the dead who had been mistreated in some way might linger to terrify the living.

Fetlar has examples of the migratory legend ML 4025 Unbaptised Child Receives a Name. Lawrence Williamson knew a version, "in a Fetlar legend two bairns used to sit on the adjacent dyke and greet till the minister went and christened them" (Johnson

1971: 112). Jeemsie Laurenson told the following second hand memorate version:

> Gilbert Laurenson was a fearless man who had the gift of second sight. He was salvaging driftwood on the beach at Gruting when he heard bairns [children] crying. He turned round and saw two naked boys. They had died without being named, so he named them Joseph and Benjamin. They thanked him and disappeared. Gilbert told the story himself.

This legend is part of the Nordic dead-child revenant legend corpus which has been studied by a number of scholars including Juha Pentikäinen (1968). Bo Almqvist (1991:160) has suggested that these legends probably originated in Norway between the 12th and mid-14th century. There are Scottish examples, but he has argued the vector of borrowing was from Norway to Scotland, via the Northern Isles. Yet again we have evidence for the Nordic character of Fetlar folklore.

Sometimes the dead were believed to interact with the living as revenant corpses and at other times as spirits. The last two stories in this collection provide examples of both. The first story is an example of E 415.4 Dead cannot rest till debts are paid. It was told by Brucie Henderson:

> Smith, a respectable merchant, charged a widow, who had five children, four times over for a lispund of meal when she could not afford to pay for it. When Smith died, he was streiked [stretched] out in the house, which is now a ruin. His corpse rose up and confessed that he could get no rest as he had cheated the woman, who had prayed to hear from the merchant before he died.

The last story concerns a ghost who demanded his boots which had been stolen from his body. It was told by Jeemsie Laurenson, who also described the location of the grave, referred to as the Dutchman's grave, near Funzie beach. Dead bodies washed up by the sea, provided yet another thing to fear. They were buried just above the high water line where they were found. There are several such graves around the coast of Fetlar.

About 200 years ago people in Fetlar salvaging wood saw the body of a seaman floating on top of a capstan bar. They took the body ashore to bury it, but thought it a pity to lose the good Wellington boots the man was wearing. But an old man warned that it was bad to steal from the dead, so they buried him with his fine boots. However, one man dug up the body, took the boots and put them in his barn. Later on he was thrashing corn with a flail by the light of a colly [simple oil lamp] when the light went out. This happened several times until, suspecting that boys were playing tricks with him, he set the colly down on the sheaves and watched. He saw a withered hand put out the colly. He went outside and saw the dead Dutchman, who accused him of stealing the boots and leaving him with cold feet in the grave. The crofter offered to give him the boots back but the Dutchman was only a spirit and said that the man would have to go and put them back on his feet. The man did so and passed the grave all his life without seeing or hearing anything. The man who had the experience swore it was true till his dying day.

The rich folklore heritage of Fetlar reveals a world only recently departed, a world where people struggled to survive by farming marginal land and pitting themselves against the dangers of the sea. A land of limited good where evil intent could bring disaster. A world inhabited by supernatural beings, both on land and sea, beings who on the whole tended to be malign.

For the visitor, perhaps the most fascinating thing about Fetlar is that, despite depopulation and an abandoned air, the supernatural geography has been preserved. One can visit Funzie where the Vikings may have made their first landfall. One can still walk on

Stackaberg, where Baabie Murray visited the trows. The Finniegirt still stands as evidence of supernatural power and the petrified remains of the trows still remain as the Haltadance stone settings. The sea still laps at Fetlar's cliffs, selkies still watch the shores and perhaps monsters still frequent the deep. Further yet lie the misty mountains of Norway home to the magic working Finns.

For the cultural historian, Fetlar's stories reveal the survival of an identifiably Nordic folklore dialect, for want of a better word. There are many clear connections with the folklore of Norway, the Faroes and Iceland, from the Finns to the Black Book, as well as with Scotland and Ireland. Fetlar provides ample evidence to support Almqvist's statement that "the Norse character of Shetland and Orkney can hardly be over-rated." (1991: 3) However, the folklore and the stories of Fetlar are also clearly Shetlandic, forged in a particular place – a small island surrounded by a savage sea.

References

Almqvist, B. 1990. Of Mermaids and Marriages. Seamus Heaney's 'Maighdean Mara' and Nuala Ní Dhomhnaill's 'an Mhaighdean Mhara' in the light of Folk Tradition. In: *Béaloideas* 58, pp. 1-74.

Almqvist, B. 1991. Crossing the Border: A Sampler of Irish Migratory Legends about the Supernatural. In: *Béaloideas*, pp. 219-278.

Almqvist, B. 1991. *Viking Ale: Studies in folklore contacts between the Northern and Western worlds*. E. Ni Dhuibhne et al. (Eds.). Aberystwyth: Boethius Press.

Black, G. F. 1903. *County Folklore Vol.III Examples of Printed Folk-lore concerning the Orkney and Shetland Islands*. N. W. Thomas (Ed.). London: David Nutt.

Blix, D. 1965. *Draugen Skreik: Tradisjon fra Lofoten*. Oslo: Universitetsforlaget (Norsk Folkeminnelags Skrifter, 93).

Boberg, I. M. 1934. *Sagnet om den Store Pans Død*. København: Levin & Munksgaards Forlag.

Bruford, A. 1978. A Host of Fairies. In: *Tocher* 28.

Bruford, A. 1997. Trolls, Hillfolk, Finns and Picts: The Identity of the Good Neighbors in Orkney and Shetland. In: P. Narvaez (Ed.), *The Good People: New Fairylore Essays*. Lexington: The University Press of Kentucky, pp. 116-141

Bø, O. 1987. *Trollmakter og godvette : overnaturlige vesen i norsk folketru*. Oslo: Det Norske Samlaget.

Catton, J. 1838. *The History and Description of the Shetland Islands*. London.

Christiansen, R. 1958. *The Migratory Legends: a proposed list of types with a systematic catalogue of Norwegian variants*. Helsinki: Suomalainen Tiedeakatemia (Folklore Fellowship Communications, 175).

Christiansen, R. (Ed.). 1964. *Folktales of Norway*. Chicago: The University of Chicago Press.

Christiansen, R. T. 1922. *Kjaetten paa Dovre*. Kristiania.

Faulkes, A. 1966. Rauðúlfs þáttr. A Study. In: *Studia Islandica* 25.

Fossenius, M. 1943. Sägnerna om trollen Finn och Skalle som byggmästare. In: *Folkkultur. Meddelanden från Lunds universitets folkminnesarkiv* 3, pp. 5-144.

Foster, G. M. 1965. Peasant Society and the Image of Limited Good. In: *American Anthropologist New Series* 27(2), pp. 293-315.

Gordon, J. 1791-1799. United Parishes or North Yell and Fetlar. In: *The Statistical Account of Scotland*, pp. 548-561.

Grydehøj, A. 2008. Nothing but a shepherd and his dog: social and economic effects of depopulation in Fetlar, Shetland. In: *Shima* 2(2), pp. 56-72.

Grydhøj, A. 2009. *Historiography of Picts, Vikings, Scots, and Fairies and Its Influence on Shetland*. A thesis presented for the degree of PhD in Ethnology and Folklore at the University of Aberdeen.

Hayes, K.J. 1997. *Folklore and Book Culture*. Knoxville: University of Tennessee.

Henderson, L. & Cowan, E. J. 2001. *Scottish Fairy Belief*. East Linton: Tuckwell Press.

Hibbert, S. 1822. *A Description of the Shetland Islands Comprising an Account of their Scenery, Antiquities, and Superstitions*. Edinburgh: Archibald Constable and Co.

Hofberg, H. 1890. *Swedish Fairy tales*. Chicago: Belford-Clarke & Co.

Jakobsen, J. 1897. *The Dialect and Place Names of Shetland*. Lerwick: T. & J. Manson.

Jakobsen, J. 1898-1901. *Færøske Folkesagn og Æventyr Udgiven for Samfund til Udgivelse af Gammel Nordisk Litteratur*. Kobenhavn: Mollers Boktrykkeri.

Jakobsen, J. (Ed.) 1928. *An Etymological Dictionary of the Norn Language in Shetland*, vol. 1. London & Copenhagen.

Jennings, A. 2007. Something funny about Funzie. In: *The New Shetlander* 242.

Johnsen, O. A. & Helgason, J. (Eds.). 1930-1941. *Saga Óláfs konungs hins helga*. Oslo.

Johnson, L. G. 1971. *Laurence Williamson of Mid-Yell*. Lerwick: The Shetland Times.

Kvideland, R. & Sehmsdorf, H. (Eds.). 1988. *Scandinavian Folk Belief and Legend*. Minneapolis: University of Minnesota Press.

Laurenson, J. J. 1964. Notes on Fetlar. In: T. A. Robertson & J. J. Graham (Eds.), *Shetland Folk Book* 4, pp. 49-54.

Mac Carthaigh, C. 1991. Midwife to the Fairies (ML 5070): The Irish variants in their Scottish and Scandinavian perspective. In: *Béaloideas*, pp. 133-143.

Mac Cárthaigh, C. 1992-1993. The Ship-Sinking Witch. A Maritime Folk Legend from North-West Europe. In: *Béaloideas*, pp. 60-61, 267-286.

MacDonald, D. A. 1994-1995. Supernatural Legends in Scotland. In: *Béaloideas*, pp. 62-63, 29-78.

Marwick, E. W. 1975. *The Folklore of Orkney and Shetland*. London: B.T. Batsford.

Milnes, G. C. 2007. *Signs, Cures and Witchery: German Appalachian Folklore*. University of Tennessee Press.

Mitchell, S. A. 2011. *Witchcraft and Magic in the Nordic Middle Ages*. Philadelphia: University of Pennsylvania Press.

Nicolson, J. 1920. *Folk-Tales and Legends of Shetland*. Edinburgh: Thomas Allan & Sons.

Pálsson, H., & Edwards, P. 1985. *Seven Viking Romances*. Harmondsworth: Penguin.

Pentikäinen, J. 1968. *The Nordic Dead-Child Tradition. Nordic Dead-Child Beings. A Study in Comparative Religion*. Helsinki: Suomalainen Tiedeakatemia (Folklore Fellowship Communications, 202).

Phelpstead, C. (Ed.). 2001. *A History of Norway and The Passion and Miracles of the Blessed Olafr*. Transl. D. Kunin. London: Viking Society for Northern Research.

Robertson, J. D. (Ed.). 1991. *An Orkney Anthology: Selected Works of Ernest Walker Marwick* (Vol. 1). Edinburgh: Scottish Academic Press.

Shaw, P., & Bruford, A. 1975. James John Laurenson. In: *Tocher* 19, pp. 81-105.

Shetland Folk Book (Vol. 2). 1951. Lerwick: The Shetland Times Ltd.

Spence, J. 1899. *Shetland Folklore*. Lerwick: Johnson & Greig.

Strömbäck, D. 1970. Some Notes on the Nix in Older Nordic Tradition. In: *Nordic Literature and Folklore Studies: Essays in Honor of Francis Lee Utley*. J. Mandel & B. Rosenberg (Eds.). New Brunswick & New Jersey: Rutgers University Press, pp. 245-256.

Thompson, S. 1977. *The Folktale*. Berkley and Los Angeles: University of California Press.

Wallace, R. 1883. *A Description of the Isles of Orkney: reprinted from the Original Edition of 1693*. Edinburgh: William Brown.

Varner, G. R. 2004. *Menhirs, Dolmen, and Circles of Stone: The Folklore and Magic of Sacred Stone*. Algora Publishing.

Williamson, H. 1957. A Fetlar Legend. In: T. A. Robertson & J. J. Graham (Eds.), *Shetland Folk Book* 3, pp. 54-55.

Williamson, L. 1957. Old Verses from Fetlar and Yell, Shetland. In: T.A. Robertson & J. J. Graham (eds.), *Shetland Folk Book* 3, pp. 1-16.

Recordings

Search *Tobar an Dualchais* http://www.tobarandualchais.co.uk for:

Catherine Mary Anderson - Selkies

Catherine Mary Anderson - Witch in form of Seal

Jeemsie Laurenson - Winjadepla

Jeemsie Laurenson - Magic working Witch 1

Jeemsie Laureson - Kirsty Ganson

Jeemsie Laurenson - Unbaptised Child Receives name 1

Jeemsie Laurenson - Dutchmans' Boots

Brucie Henderson - Dead Cannot rest till Debts Paid

Chapter 3
"He Met His Own Funeral Procession": The Year Walk Ritual in Swedish Folk Tradition

Tommy Kuusela
Stockholm University, Sweden

Introduction

The belief in prophetic signs bound to specific and important dates can be seen all over Europe as early as Medieval times, with weather and harvest divinations being the most common kinds (Cameron 2013: 65-67). In Sweden, one oracular method was a ritual known as year walk, and those who ventured on this perilous journey were known as year walkers. Success meant that the omen-seeker could acquire knowledge of the following year; it was a ritual that sought answers regarding the unbearable uncertainty of being. Year walk (or annual walk) is known in Swedish as *årsgång*, with regional and lexical variations: *ådergång, julagång, ödegång, adergång, dödsgång, sjukyrkegång*, and so on. Although the term *årsgång* has a southern Swedish pattern of distribution (Götaland), similar practices, as well as the same motifs in different types of folk legends, are common and can be found throughout the Nordic countries. Most of the source material comes from, but is not limited to, southern Sweden, and dates approximately from the 17th Century to the first half of the 20th Century.

In this paper, I will examine the Swedish folk tradition (Swedish should be understood in a linguistic sense, not in a geographical or political sense) known as year walk and will try to fit it into a pattern of other known folk customs. My source material consists of four older accounts by Petter Rudebeck (c. 1700), Petrus Gaslander (c. 1750), Johan J. Törner (c. 1737-1787), and Ernst Moritz Arndt (1807) as well as collections by folklorists and hundreds of records drawn from Swedish folklore archive cabinets, predominantly from the collections in Gothenburg (Dialekt-, ortnamns- och folkminnesarkivet), Stockholm (Nordiska museet), Uppsala (Dialekt-, språk- och folkminnesinstitutet), and Lund (Folklivsarkivet). To my knowledge, a presentation of Year walk has never been written in English before: Therefore I have translated all of the cited narratives into English.

The oldest records of year walk

The oldest account of year walk can be found in *Småländska Antiqviteter* (*Antiquities from Småland*), a manuscript produced around 1697-1700, which is now held in the National Library of Sweden. The curious text was written by Petter Rudebeck (1660-1710), a quartermaster who lived in the province of Småland in southern Sweden. One chapter deals directly with the year walk custom. This is interesting, not least because he describes the custom as old, and if we consider when it was written, it ought to describe a custom that was well-known in southern Sweden, at least since the 1600s. I have not found any older records that mention year walk although there are older references to different kinds of omens and oracular rituals associated with Christmas.

Petrus Gaslander (1680-1758) was a vicar who had a great interest in collecting rural Småland's customs and beliefs. One of his works, *Beskriftning om Svenska Allmogens Sinneslag och Seder...* (*Character and Customs of the Peasantry...*), was published after his death in 1774 and includes a brief description of year walk. (There has been some debate as to whether his son Johannes Gaslander wrote parts of the work.) The description of year walk is connected with Christmas Eve, where it is said that if someone before first light on Christmas Eve goes into a forest without saying a word, without looking back, without looking into a fire, without food and drink, and so far that the crowing of a cock cannot be heard, they can walk on church roads and see all of the funeral processions of the coming year, and by looking at the fields, they will see how the harvest will turn out and if and where there will be fires as well as other things that will come to pass. Gaslander mentions that this is called year walk and that it is an ancient custom that is no longer practiced (Gaslander 1982: 22).

Johan Johannis Törner (1712-1790), a lector and provost from Linköping, wrote *Samling af widskeppelser* (*Collection of Superstitions*), a large collection of notes on all kinds of rural customs and beliefs, which he collected over a span of fifty years. He mentions year walk on two occasions. His first note has to do with Midsummer: someone who does not speak or eat on Midsummer Eve, who sits up throughout the night, and then walks around the fields and meadows – that person will hear and see what will happen the next year, will see corpses, his spouse, children, good or bad harvests, killings, etc. This is called year walk. Some people do this on Christmas Eve, *Persmässonatten* on 29 June, or *Lucia* on 13 December (Törner 1946: 74, 76). The second reference is rather short. He says that it is still known that during Christmas Eve, people use prognostication to look for omens of the future. In pre-Christian times, this was known as year walk (Törner 1946: 151). Sadly, he does not describe the technique in detail but gives many other examples of omen-seeking connected to important calendar days.

Ernst Moritz Arndt (1769-1860) was born on the island of Rügen, an area that was a part of Swedish Pomerania between 1648 and 1815. He wrote his travel memoirs *Reise durch Schweden im Jahr 1804* (*Travels through Sweden in the Year 1804*) in four volumes, based on his travels from 3 November 1803, until 6 September 1804. He travelled through many districts of Sweden and wrote avidly and meticulously on what he saw and learned. His descriptions of customs, legends, and rural life are therefore of great value. In one chapter, he focuses on Swedish Christmas traditions, not from a specific district but from Sweden as a whole. He mentions that on Christmas night, people try to get a glimpse of the future year and that this is something people did more in the past because, in his days, people think of it as a superstition or something that was done because it was traditional, without any sense of gravity. He says that in the past, some people went as quietly as possible to the forest, without saying a word: they did not look back and had made sure to stay away from food and drink and avoided looking into fires earlier in the day, and they made sure to be so far away that they could not hear a cock crow. When the sun rose, they were on the church road where the next years' funeral procession could be seen. They would also see if the harvest would be good or bad by looking at the fields, meadows, and grazing grounds, and they could see if a fire was going to break out during the next year. This was known as year walk (Arndt 1994: 44).

Distinctive calendar days and omens
In preindustrial and rural Sweden, important calendar days were integrated with numerous and varied folk beliefs. The period that started with the preparations for Christmas and ended with New Year was considered an important, as well as the most dangerous, time of the year. During this time, it was believed that supernatural forces were particularly active, magic formulas worked best, and omens and portents became observable. The days of Christmas were omen-days, and the dead were given free rein to leave their dwellings to roam the Earth and visit the living (Weiser-Aall 1963:

9-10). At the culmination of the calendar year, when nights grew longer and the temperature dropped, Christmas night marked the passing of one year and the beginning of another. At least, this was the case from Medieval times until the 17th Century, but old traditions and customs in relation to Christmas persisted in the countryside for a long period of time (Celander 1928: 205; Bergstrand 1939: 14). Throughout this season – a period that can be considered liminal – dark forces and supernatural beings became active. It started with *Lussenatten* (Sw. *Lusse, Lucifersnatten*) or St Lucy's Day, on 13 December. In places where *Lusse* was not celebrated, it was on *Tomasnatten*, the longest night of the year (21 December, coinciding with Winter Solstice). Closely related with beliefs in these supernatural beings are notions of omens and portents as well as techniques to see what is hidden.

In Europe, there is an old belief that the spirits of the dead wander the earth during the 12-day Christmas cycle (the days between Christmas and Epiphany). If the spirits entered a house and were given food offerings, they could bring luck and prosperity to the household. According to Claude Lecouteux, this can be seen as a calendar-based rite that belongs to a system of beginnings: whatever happens on this date predicts happenings over the next year. A similar custom was even celebrated by the Greeks and Romans, where a certain table was set for the deceased. Set tables with gifts or offerings for the dead are recorded from the entire Middle Ages in clerical literature, for example by St Boniface, the pseudo-Augustine, Césaire of Arles, and Yves de Chartes (Lecouteux 2011: 17-18).

During the 19th Century, people in the southern provinces of Sweden used to eat their Christmas meal on two occasions: the first at Christmas Eve, consisting of beer, meat, fish, porridge, and pastry, and a second at around midnight, with lighter food such as butter, bread, and turnips (Celander 1928: 176). Descriptions vary, but an interesting detail is that some of the food was never cleared from the table: it was intentionally left for the dead who were believed to visit the farms during the night. Other records mention that the food should never run out, which can be explained as an oracular belief that a plentiful table meant that the next year would also be abundant with food (Celander 1928: 204-208). Different rituals and customs became associated with these meals. In records, primarily from western Sweden, it is mentioned that before eating his porridge, the farmer hurried outside and circled the cabin counter-clockwise three times. This was supposed to give a glimpse of the future. Sometimes the farmer brought a porridge sceptre (Sw. *grötkräkla*) or another object with a hole or some kind of opening in it through which he could look (a wedding ring, a black silk scarf, a piece of round bread, etc.) and held it in front of his eyes. If this was done properly, it was thought that he could hear and see things that were otherwise hidden. If he looked through a window, he could see who would die the following year; they, or their shadows, would be seated headless at the table. If the one who did this was unmarried, there was a chance of getting a glimpse of a future bride or groom. Not every record mentions a counter-clockwise pattern around the house; some just say that the walk should be performed backwards (Sw. *avigt*), away from the window, and that it was forbidden to speak to anyone (Celander 1928: 222-223; Wallin 1941: 103).

The practice of walking counter-clockwise around a building (or another object) is known in Swedish folk tradition as *kringgång*. Curt Wallin considered this to be the antecedent of the year walk-tradition. The difference between the customs is that *kringgång*, as practiced in the manner just described, was usually meant to give omens associated with the household or closest family, and that the extent of the walk was limited (Wallin 1941: 102-3). I disagree with Wallin on this and agree with Carl Herman Tillhagen, who instead thinks that *kringgång* around the house at Christmas night is a watered down form of an older and more complex oracular ritual (Tillhagen 1980: 156). For someone who went on a year walk, the area that he or she was required to walk extended to three or seven churches, to three crossroads, fields, church yards, or a similar distance. In place of omens involving one's immediate household, a year walker tried to glean knowledge of what would happen the coming year, regarding not only the closest family but also the whole village or parish. Both churches and crossroads can be considered liminal places – they are borders between worlds – and as such are intimately connected with the dead, with supernatural beings, and with hidden, esoteric knowledge. Year walk can thus be described as a special technique of divination that attempts to answer fundamental questions for the seemingly random events of life.

The first steps of the ritual
Year walk, according to the records in the Swedish Folklore Archives, was performed on certain days of the year, usually during winter and Christmas Eve, but there are records of similar practices taking place at Midsummer, Easter, *Tomasmässonatten* on 21 December, *Staffansnatten* on 26 December, New Year's Eve, and *Trettondagsnatten* (Twelfth Night) on 5 January. Most accounts indicate that year walk took place at midnight, with slight variations, but they agree that the ritual should be executed before the sun rises or the cook crows (Bergstrand 1939: 14-15; Wallin 1941: 108). The oldest records (Rudebeck, Gaslander, Törner, and Arndt) state that the person who wants to go on a year walk has to make certain preparations and observe a set of guidelines. The year walker should not eat (at least not later than the afternoon), not look at or into any source of bright light or fire (if fire was seen, it

had to be neutralised by making a new fire with flint and steel outdoors), not mention the intention of going on a year walk to anyone, not speak or reply to anyone, not look back, not be terrified or laugh at anything that was encountered, no matter how frightening or comical (Rudebeck 1997: 274). Basically, a good method was to brace oneself by entering a secluded and dark room without food or any kind of social contact. If these rules were followed, the year walker became sensitive to the supernatural, but if they were not, dangerous things could happen.

Before we turn to the next part of the ritual, I will give some further examples on how to prepare for a year walk, based on the records from the Swedish Folklore Archives. One informant from Mårdaklev parish in the district of Västergötland says:

> One way was to leave the house and go away before the light of day and to go so far in the woods that on the entire day (Christmas Eve) neither dog barks nor cock crows could be heard. When returning home, no words ought to be said and teeth's ought not to be shown. After supper, The Lord's Prayer ought to be read quietly to oneself and it should be done so backwards (IFGH 3304: 1).

Another informant says that preparations were done by going out into the woods on the morning of Christmas Eve where no food or contact with other humans was allowed (IFGH 3314: 13).

How the ritual was accomplished

A great deal of folk belief and practice centres on time, with rigid temporal limits, and space, with boundaries of all kinds. The year walk must be performed at an explicit time and carried out before a certain hour, for example before sunrise or at midnight, and on a particular night (Christmas Eve, New Year's Eve, Midsummer's Night, and so on). The objective is in most cases to get to the parish church or a cluster of churches: some records mention three or seven churches. A couple of records note various destinations such as a forest, crossroads, or secluded areas far from other human beings. The year walker's senses become heightened and open to the supernatural world, which means that there will be obstacles on the way that can be anything from strange visions to close encounters with supernatural beings. The movement should be in a certain direction (usually counter-clockwise) and done a certain number of times (as a rule, these instructions apply when the year walker arrives at a destination, be it a church or somewhere else). A year walker must usually travel alone by foot, but some records mention pairs, and in rare cases that three could walk together (IFGH 4979:24). In one record, the year walker is allowed to ride a horse (E.U. 4265: 1212).

As noted above, the omen-seeker must usually visit a number of churches, circle them a certain number of times, and follow a pattern: for example so that each time he or she passes the church door, he or she has to breathe or peek into the keyhole. Looking through the keyhole could reveal strange sights, which in turn could expose glimpses of the following year. If there was a service, empty benches meant that a certain person was going to die: sometimes the service was a funeral, a wedding, or other special occasion. In some records, the dead occupy the church, and if someone was among them, it was a sure sign that the person was going to die during the next year. If a year walker attended the service, he or she could learn things that had to do with future events. One record mentions that the year walker had to read 'The Devil's blessing' (Sw. *Skams välsignelse*) at the church door three times and at the same time breathed through the keyhole of the church door. This was, of course, dangerous, and a year walker might become cursed (Sw. *osalig*). By doing this, premonitions of the future appeared (IFGH 4073: 34-35). One record mentions that a year walker got a forceful slap in his face right in front of the church door and lost an eye (IFGH 3488: 19). A slap in the face is a common motif in folk legends when someone angers the supernatural. Similar records mention loss of sanity or that the year walker's head become distorted (Bergstrand 1939: 25). From Visby, on the island of Gotland, there is a description of a failed year walk. The person had to run around Visby Cathedral (Sw. *Storkyrkan*) three times at midnight but was unsuccessful and disappeared (IFGH 849: 10).

A common motif is that the year walker encounters a funeral procession (Type A40-41 in af Klintberg 2010: 32), either on the road or in the church yard, and learns who will die in the community during the following year. In some of the descriptions, the year walker finds out by asking the procession about the identity of the departed (or by other means) and learns that it is none other than the one who asked the question. This is a recurrent motif that must have been truly alarming and means that a year walker must be audacious and prepared for anything. The graveyard could be filled with all kinds of activity. The graves might be open, songs (usually psalms) could be heard from the graves, the dead could be roaming about (those who have committed suicide were especially dangerous and could be hostile), and fresh graves that otherwise did not exist could show the walker who would die.

In some of the examples I have given, a year walker was supposed to read the Lord's Prayer backwards or use other means that seem to be under the direct influence of the Devil. One record from Uppsala mentions that the year walker was sworn to the Devil and had to go on a year walk every year, otherwise the Devil would come and bang wildly on his door, demanding an explanation (ULMA K, A4). This was pointed out by Carl-Martin Bergstrand, who adds more examples. One such account comes from the Karl-Gustav parish in the province of Västergötland, where a year walker is

[68]

standing in front of the church door and summons the Devil, who comes and reveals what will happen in the following year. He also mentions a record in which the year walker never seemed to run out of money, which is a sure sign that a contract with the Devil is involved. He also points out that many of the records do not give the impression that the informants saw year walk as something pagan. The Devil or the black arts are rarely mentioned. Most walks were practiced during a time of year when supernatural beings where lively, and people might very well have considered those nights as belonging to them (Bergstrand 1939: 25-26).

Many descriptions specify that if a year walker completed his or her expedition in the right fashion, it was on the way back that omens and portents started to appear. As might be expected when it comes to folk narratives, the descriptions are contradictory. Many accounts speak of the tradition as something that could be repeated year after year. Every year, the year walker's powers grew, and on his seventh or ninth year, there was a chance to gain permanent second sight or other extraordinary abilities. There is one record from Tårsås parish, in the district of Småland, that states that one particular man, described as short and ugly, functioned as a wise man in his community because he had gifts of healing as a result of his year walks, but it also says that the man had to continue with a walk yearly, but when he turned 85 years old, he was too weak, and for this reason he perished (E.U. 3330:70).

The purpose of the ritual
Why would anyone risk the safety of home and go on a walk that was considered dangerous? Rudebeck describes the purposes of the year walk (similar details are given in younger accounts):

An old custom in Småland has been to search for all of the year's properties and learn how to observe what will happen in the following year. How the crops will turn out, who will live and die in the farmstead, if there will be significant death, if someone from abroad will visit, if there is reason to fear war and unlucky fate, if there will be fire or lack of water in the farms or villages, if wicked sorcery will be performed, if fishing or hunting will be good, and much more (Rudebeck 1997: 274).

People have always desired to get a glimpse of the future, and most of the questions naturally circle around basic human needs and fears; life, livelihood, marriage, and death. Marriage and the wish to know one's future bride or groom are not mentioned by Rudebeck, Gaslander, or Arndt, but they can be found in Törner and many of the younger descriptions. It must have been a part of similar oracular traditions from an early stage. In his book on Christmas traditions in Scandinavia and Swedish Finland, Hilding Celander mentions a manuscript from Valders, dated to the late 17th Century, which can be taken as a confirmation of this:

On Christmas Eve, widows and maidens shall fast until the sun goes down, stars glimmer in the sky, tablecloth lain out, candles and food set on the table. Then they shall, those who have fasted, go to the table and take something with their mouth and something with their hand, then go backwards out through the door, sit somewhere out in the yard, wherever they want, and chew on the food that is in their mouth. During this time they should carefully pay heed if there can be heard knocking or rumbling somewhere, and carefully take note of that place from whence the sound seem to come. For from that place, whence the sound comes from, a suitor and fiancé will come to the one who hears the sound before the year ends (Celander 1928: 224-225).

This description of a marriage divination offers a clear parallel to some narratives of year walkers who wanted to find out about their future brides or fiancés. It does not mention the same kind of ritual, but many of its elements are comparable – it takes place on Christmas Eve, the practitioner must fast and is forbidden to speak of what happens, a walk is performed backwards, the ritual takes place outdoors, and the omens are sensory. Numerous accounts found in the younger material mention that the outcome of this oracular tradition is a glimpse of one's future companion. One even mentions a sailor who walked around the stern of his ship counter-clockwise and thus got to see his future bride (IFGH 4351: 8). Another method is to go naked around a well three times counter-clockwise and three times clockwise (IFGH 4446:2).

Celander mentions another custom connected with fishing luck from Norway that is similar to some aspects of year walk. Apparently fishermen from the coast of Norway marked the spot where bubbles appeared in a wooden cask filled with sea water. This was brought back home at Christmas Eve and placed at or under a table during Christmas Eve and covered with a piece of bread or something similar. The next morning, before speaking with anyone, it was measured where the bubbles where thickest. That was believed to represent the fjord where fishing would be most plentiful the following year. Celander also suggests that similar traditions can be found in Norrland of northern Sweden, but in those parts the outcome is to measure how the harvest will turn out (Celander 1928: 219; cf. Feilberg, II, 1904: 134). In collections of folk narratives from Norrland by Ella Odstedt there are many legends that resemble year walk, even though this name is never used. One account (No 978) says that on Midsummer's Night, it was possible to walk to a crossroads where three roads met and wait until midnight. Then a future husband or wife would appear. But it could also happen that a mouse drawing a cart with hay appeared (Odstedt 2004: 230-245).

Some year walkers had a special purpose – to become wise (Sw. *klok*), learn magic, or obtain a magical object (e.g. a grimoire, magic formulas, or a magic hat). The term *cunning* incorporates these aspects: A cunning man or woman is a prominent and numinous figure to whom ordinary people turned when they needed help, for example with healing or finding lost goods (Davies 2003; Wilby 2013: 26-31). Other year walkers wished to increase their luck for the coming year, e.g. by circling a certain church three times (IFGH 2149: 1). It was also possible to gain the ability to learn how to lock out (Sw. *låsa bort*) rats and mice (IFGH 1384: 52). A couple of accounts from Kristianopel parish in the province of Blekinge mention a unique and special purpose: year walk was performed by werewolves who wanted to get rid of their curse. Both accounts are similar, but one is more thorough:

There was an old man who was a werewolf and to get rid of his curse he had to go and look through the keyhole of three churches. On his way he met a hen that pulled a cart with hay. The hen said: 'To Mörby! To Mörby!'(Mörby is a place name) At that moment the old man laughed and became hare-lipped for the rest of his life. Not only that, he did not get rid of his foulness. This is not strange, because a werewolf, who went on a year walk, was not allowed to laugh or talk to anyone (LUF 5903, see Wallin 1941: 123).

None of the accounts mention anything involving glimpses of the future, and there are reasons – not least in the narrative style – to suspect that the motifs have become distorted. Werewolves and year walk appearing in the same account is an uncommon theme and might have been parts of local folk narratives, where the informants have mixed up year walk with legends of people who tried to get rid of their lycanthropy. Maybe it was told as a joke, in the same vein as the ones Arndt mentioned much earlier. According to Ella Odstedt, in her great study of Swedish werewolf traditions, both accounts come from the same informant and can therefore not be taken as proof of a distinctive variant of a tradition shared in the community (Odstedt 2012: 184, n. 152).

Dangers and supernatural interference

As mentioned above, Christmas-time was associated with increased activities by supernatural beings. This is evident from many descriptions where they clearly tried to hinder the year walker, while the hazards and obstacles could become increasingly demanding. A year walker was not allowed to laugh, stray from the path, or look back, and he or she needed to be prepared to see things that could seem comical, alarming, or baneful. The regulation to stay quiet and not laugh is also common in many treasure-seeker legends. One motif found in year walk and treasure hunt accounts is that of a lame hen or something similar pulling a hay-cart, which manages to get the treasure-hunter or omen-seeker to laugh or talk, with the result that the silence is broken, and the quest fails. The motif of a burning house or village can also be found in both types, where the treasure-hunter or omen-seeker breaks off his quest because he sees a fire, only to discover that it was an optical illusion (Lindow 1982: 264-266; Type A43, V61, V67 in af Klintberg 2010: 385-386). These descriptions can be found in Rudebeck: if there would be a war the coming year, a year walker might experience loud chopping noises from the woods or see soldiers hurrying on the roads to the sounds of horns and pipes. If there would be a bad harvest, a small number of people could be seen on the croplands binding and carrying small sheaves whereas others would sit on heaps of stones, grieving and sighing. Fires and floods could be seen over the farms that would have a tough year. Most of the omens described are inauspicious, but there are also good omens where small men are seen carrying big sheaves.

Rudebeck also remarks that all kinds of supernatural beings roamed the lands during a year walk. He points out that a year walker might experience exhilarating or comical events, but laughing or smiling was prohibited because if the year walker did so, his or her mouth could be fixed in that position forever (Rudebeck 1997: 274-275). This could be easier said than done as some of the narratives are truly hilarious. A variety of supernatural beings did everything they could to break the year walker's concentration. One account states that the year walker saw a big hay-cart drawn by two small rats and found it both strange and amusing because it was the middle of winter. He had a hard time not laughing, but it got worse; one of the rats slipped on the ice and fell on his back while farting so loudly that it could be heard across the whole parish. At that moment, the year walker burst into laughter, and the vision disappeared, which meant his quest was for naught (Wallin 1941: 130).

Some beings are more dangerous than others: the most terrifying being a year walker could meet was a big sow with sharp teeth and burning eyes called Gloson (see below). Another record from the district of Västergötland says that both Gloson and the Hel-horse could be seen close to the churchyard wall (IGH 3454: 5). In this case, a Hel-horse is probably the church grim in the form of a horse. In one account from Vårvik, in the province of Dalsland, the informant Ragnar Johansson says that a year walker could see an assortment of beings in the church yard: werewolves, revenants, trolls, and rats. If this was managed and the walk completed, it was possible to look into the future. If someone went on a year walk for nine years in a row, that person became "all-knowing" (IFGH 1732: 12). One record from Långasjö parish in the province of Småland states that it was of the utmost importance to stay calm and not look back or stray from the path, otherwise there was a risk of contracting a serious disease (E.U. 2591:687). In folk belief, it is usually considered dangerous to be touched by supernatural beings such as ghosts and revenants, which could cause a foul and sudden disease (Sw. *gastkramad*, cf. Hagberg 1937: 610-616).

On 25 December, the dead gathered in church and celebrated *julotta*, which in earlier days was a popular service held in Swedish churches in celebration of the birth of Christ, early or slightly before dawn. (cf. Type 4015 'The Midnight Mass of the Dead' in Christiansen 1992: 61). This particular *julotta* overlapped with the year walk. Many records mention that a year walker came to a graveyard and saw light coming out from the church. If the person entered or looked inside, he or she could see that the church benches were packed with the dead – skeletons, corpses, and sometimes a revenant priest who conducted the service. The dead did not tolerate the living: in some horrifying descriptions, it is said that they had to tear something to pieces and that the best way to save oneself was to leave a piece of garment behind (Hagberg 1937: 650-661). Carl Wilhelm von Sydow remarked in a review of the aforementioned book by Hilding Celander that the *julotta* celebrated by the dead had nothing to do with year walk, but he never explained why (the statement was repeated by him later on). The reason for his critique of Celander might be due to a tension that was growing between the two, which made von Sydow lash out with groundless statements as facts. This was typical of his polemical style (cf. Drobin 1983; Bringéus 2006:126-127, 150-152; Skott 2010: 73-75). There are many records that link year walk with this particular *julotta*, and the link is clearly made by the informants as well (Bergstrand 1937: 120; 1939: 26).

Gloson and the church grim

Numerous records mention a terrible ghost pig called 'Gloson', which alongside the church grim were feared enemies of a year walker. Rudebeck, Arndt, Törner, and Gaslander do not mention Gloson, but Rudebeck speaks of an old man who shows himself on the seventh year walk. This man is clearly supernatural and is described as sitting on a horse with fire coming out of his neck and carrying a stick with rune carvings in his mouth (Rudebeck 1997: 275). I think that this man, who echoes notions of Odin, fills the same purpose as later descriptions of Gloson. The name *Gloson* might be derived from the verb *att glo* (to stare) and *so, sugga* (sow), but a great variety of names are attached to this being (*luffesoen, gloppsoan, gluppson, glopsuggan, gloffson, lyckoso, gluffsoen,* and so on). According to Curt Wallin (the records I have read support this), most accounts tend to focus on the Gloson's swift movement, and a number of records mention that the sow's whole body is covered with glowing eyes (Wallin 1941: 125). Descriptions of Gloson vary and are usually filled with all kinds of horror motifs, a common theme being that she is a big horrible sow with her back in the shape of a razor-sharp saw, but in some records it is said that she could also carry a year walker far away on her back (Type C201 in af Klintberg 2010: 81). A common motif is that Gloson runs at the year walker at full speed and seeks to come between the year walker's legs and cleave the walker in two. One means of protection was to cross one's legs (other methods include feeding Gloson certain prepared objects, such as seven-year-old nuts; throwing a fishing net over her; or using knowledge of the black arts). Other records describe Gloson as anthropomorphic, with a pig's head and big tusks. A theme that can be found in many records is that Gloson carries a rune stick or paper roll in her mouth, and if the year walker manages to grab this, either through swiftness or by overturning her, the item could be used to instruct the year walker in sorcery (Wallin 1941: 126-129).

The church grim or church genius (Sw. *kyrkogrim, kyrkevar, kyrkorå, kyrkodrake,* etc.) is usually believed to be the first being – typically an animal (horse, lamb, calf, swine, hen, etc.) but sometimes even a human – that is buried when a new church is built. In some legends, it is the first person who dies at one year of age who becomes a church grim and guards the premises of the church yard. This being is a natural enemy of the year walker, who had to pass the graveyard and circle the church (cf. Pape 1946).

Is the year walk tradition a pre-Christian survival?
Many of the descriptions mentioned above refer to year walk as an ancient tradition. The well-known Swedish folklorist Gunnar-Olof Hyltén-Cavallius described year walk in the same way, as a remnant that dated back to a pre-Christian past:

> The ancient heathen folk practice, that in Wärend since olden days was known by the names to *go year walk* and *go midsummer walk*. [...] can generally be considered, one of the most remarkable remnants from a heathen age and of a mythical outlook that hitherto managed to preserve itself among any of the newer European peoples (Hyltén-Cavallius [1863-1864] 1972: 391).

For Hyltén-Cavallius, the recorded customs and beliefs could easily be compared with a hypothetical past and therefore with even older sources dating back to pre-Christian times. This can be viewed in a much broader perspective, where romantic notions and theories led many academics and writers to embellish their particular national history and place it on a pedestal. It fits the nationalist movements that swept through Europe in the 19th Century: for some, it was a question of trying to prove through folklore that their nations where the grandest and most exciting; for others, their hearts were intimately attached to their province, and they sought to prove that their own home-region held the oldest, the most genuine, and the most sensational folklore material (Baycroft & Hopkin 2012). It might be tempting to look upon the practice of year walk as an old survival from heathen times, but then we must find some kind of proof of its existence before the Reformation. In my opinion, there are no such fossilised pieces of quaint tradition that with certainty can be traced back to pre-Christian beliefs or practices. The church effectively suppressed all vestiges of paganism as a religion and as a mode of worship. Although there are links that connect younger folklore material with older traditions, the picture is far from uncomplicated, and the shifting of traditions can often be misleading. What characterises folklore is the tendency of traditions to change or alter shape in transmission from one generation to another. But even if details change, as well as the accepted reasons for different practices, the basic principles can remain and fall into a discernible pattern.

Although it is often stated that year walk is an ancient practice, I have actually not seen any examples of how year walk can be traced to pre-Christian or even Medieval Scandinavian traditions. Therefore, I will give a couple of samples of traditions known from Norse sources of rituals performed outdoors and associated with prophecy. Space prevents me from exploring it in depth. Predicting the future, as well as different methods for affecting or controlling it, was viewed as witchcraft and sorcery in the medieval provincial laws in Scandinavia. It was considered a short step between wishing to know the future and desiring to affect or control it. It was actually so abominable that the perpetrators of such fortune telling were severely punished by banishment and a heavy fine of 40 marks. In the Norwegian Borgarthing Law, in the older Christian law sections, it is stated: *Þæt er ubotaværk at sitia uti* "it is a felony/crime to sit out" (Halvorsen & Rindal 2008: 154). What this legislation means is that the practice of "sitting out" is strictly prohibited and cannot be atoned for with wealth: the condemned practitioners (*ubotamenn*) were barred from compensating their crimes and were normally banished, usually into pagan countries, and their property confiscated (Jørgensen 2013: 246-247). The key word *útiseta* (*sitja úti*), also known from the Norwegian Gulathing Law, is a ritual strongly associated with someone who sits outside at night, possibly on grave mounds or at crossroads, and practices, in the eyes of the law, sorcery and witchcraft. Its semantic spectrum signifies more than a night-time location, and it should be seen as an old technique for evoking spirits. Similarly strict prohibitions, with slight variations, against the ritual as a heathen practice can be found in other laws. One law condemns: *spafarar allar oc utiscætor at ueckia troll upp* "spae-journey and sitting out awakening trolls" (NGL II 265; cf. de Vries 1956: 328-330). The Old Norse compound *spáför* is interesting: the first element *spá* is the same as the archaic English and Scottish *spae* and means 'soothsaying, foretelling, or prophecy'. The second element *för* indicates a journey or travel but can also mean walk in the sense of begging (Fritzner 1954: 533). It sounds similar to year walk, and in connection with trolls, it means that the law condemns a practice associated with invoking and gaining esoteric knowledge from supernatural beings. The church was extremely critical of this practice, and one Icelandic episcopal ordinance of 1178 condemns people who: *sitja úti til fróðleiks* "sit out at night for the sake of gaining knowledge" (Samplonius 1995: 77). This ritual is a solitary nocturnal practice aimed at establishing contact with the Otherworld. Even though the law texts themselves, or rather the manuscripts, are no older than the 13th Century, they suggest that the traditions they ban are likely much older.

The Poetic Edda mentions the practice of both *útiseta* and *sitja á haugi* (see below). One of the best-known eddic poems, *Völuspá*, dated to the 10th Century, describes how the god Odin seeks out a *völva* "sibyl, prophetess" and asks her to foretell future events. In stanza 28, we read: *ein sat hón úti* "alone she held séance out in the night" (Dronke 1997: 14). The Old High German expression *hlīodarsazzo* "sitting to listen" can also be seen as a parallel to *útiseta*. The oldest occurrence of the derivate agent noun is *hleotharsazzo*, which glosses Latin *negromanticus* (cf. Meissner 1917: 100-110; Samplonius 1995: 79). There are many Old Norse texts in various genres that deal with the expression 'sitting out', usually in connection with prophecy, sorcery, awakening trolls (spirits, the dead), or as a heathen practice, and the practice can still be found in Icelandic legends as late as the 17th Century (Mitchell 2011: 161-162; Strömbäck 2000: 127-129). Dag Strömbäck divides the practice into two parts. On the one hand, the practitioner takes an active part in summoning the supernatural beings (the dead) from their Otherworld. On the other hand, the practitioner is passive and sits at crossroads, on mounds, in caves, or in other secluded places and quietly listens and observes the surroundings for signs (Strömbäck 2000: 128-129).

Another ritual is the practice of *sitja á haugi* "to sit on a barrow", which occurs frequently in the Old Norse texts and seems related to *útiseta*. Axel Olrik thinks the practice of sitting on barrows or grave mounds is connected with kingship (Olrik 1909). In my opinion, it suits a popular pattern of omen-seeking, which can be seen in both year walk and "sitting out", without any aristocratic connotations. There was always a danger with this kind of ritual, for a person who dared it might be attacked by the dead and killed or end up insane.

I will end this brief survey of Nordic traditions of "sitting out", with a 19th Century Icelandic example from Jón Árnason's collection of folk-tales. Motifs will be recognised from both the old practice of "sitting out" and year walk. In most of his tales, the ritual is most successful if done on a Midsummer's Night or, as in the following account, on New Year's Eve:

[80]

He who intended to practice 'sitting out' to gain news had to equip himself with a gray cat, a grey sheepskin, a walrus hide or the hide of an old bull, and an axe. All this the necromancer should take to a crossroads all of which led straight and unbroken to four churches. At the crossroads the person was to lie down, cover himself with the hide and tuck it in on every side so no part of the body was left visible. He is to hold the axe between his hands and stare at the edge and look neither left nor right whatever happened; nor was he to answer should someone address him. In this posture one is to lie motionless till dawn of the following day. When the necromancer had finished installing himself he started an incantation and the formulas necessary to summon the dead. Thereupon his relatives appeared, if he had any buried at one or more of the four churches which the roads led to, and they told him everything he wanted to know, both things that had come to pass and were to pass many centuries hence. If the necromancer was steadfast enough to stare at the edge of the axe, never take his eyes off it and not say a word whatever happened, he would not only remember everything the dead told him, but he could, whenever he wanted to and without any risk, receive news from them of everything he wanted to know by sitting out (Aðalsteinsson 1978: 118).

Jón Hnefill Aðalsteinsson (1978) gives many examples of soothsaying under a cloak or skin, both from Iceland and parallels from Ireland. They all mention that the soothsayer should not speak to anyone, be solitary, and usually must withdraw to a secluded setting. The quoted example above, together with older motifs related to omen-seeking and a quest for hidden knowledge, easily finds counterparts and falls in a visible pattern of many folklore traditions in agrarian societies. It is hard to prove that a tradition, known from younger sources, can be linked with pre-Christian practices.

The Swedish year walk custom is probably not a pre-Christian survival, but some of its elements are surely connected to the past and several layers of folklore and religious traditions. We must not forget that Sweden gradually became a Catholic country in the Medieval period and later converted to Protestantism in the 16th Century, but folklore elements can linger for a very long time, even survive for more than a thousand years, albeit in new forms.

Conclusion

To conclude this brief article on year walk, it might be a good idea to contextualise the ritual and place it in a fitting folkloristic framework. One thing that is clear is that people could take great steps to preserve or gain good luck and avert ill-luck, which also includes a wish to secure the prosperity of the household and, if they were unmarried, find a future spouse. It is also certain that there were all kinds of beliefs connected with the eves of major holidays. Different techniques for finding out what the future holds can be found in a great variety of records of Swedish folk tradition (cf. Tillhagen 1980). Due to concerns about how the next year would turn out, people did what they could to obtain glimpses and knowledge of the future. Societies of all times have sought to presage the future by observing things or occurrences around them. This could involve all manner of signs and omens: omens of good luck, omens of ill luck, death omens, marriage omens, weather omens, fire omens, war omens, visitation omens, omens of wealth, and so on (cf. Ó Súilleabháin 1942: 378-80).

The practice of sitting out or going to a crossroads or grave mound to learn about the future is, as we have seen, an old custom. Can the year walk be seen as a form of divination? Divination is the practice of attempting to discover the unknown or gain insight into the future by supernatural means. The Latin word *divinus* means 'one inspired by the gods', and divination might be described as any ritual and its associated tradition that is performed in order to ask a supernatural being for guidance. The practice still flourishes in the Western world in the form of fortune-tellers, tarot card reading, palmistry, tea leaf divination, and gazing into crystal balls (cf. Ellis 2004: 142–173). If we seek to outline divination into categories and see it as a system of knowledge, a good starting point is to cite Åke Hultkrantz's classification, which covers many types of divination from different cultures, including Nordic folklore material (Hultkrantz 1976: 70):

1. Passive divination

A) Spontaneous inspirational divination: supernatural forces come into direct contact with the human being, intentionally or unintentionally. It can be in waking hallucinations, dreams, or as ecstatic hallucinations.

B) Spontaneous premonitory vision (and auditions): this applies to premonitions experienced in waking hallucinations or dreams. They can be distinguished by the fact that they depict a course of events still to occur, or persons who will experience future fateful events in some way or other.

C) Spontaneous configurations to be read (Sw. *tydor*): this class refers to omina that appear unexpectedly (or essentially without foreboding) and are experienced by the person while awake.

2. Active divination

A) Active inspirational divination: this group refers to those states of inspiration (waking hallucinations, dreams, and ecstatic hallucinations), which have been prepared or provoked by the inspired person himself or herself and which result in encounters with supernatural powers. Trance experiences in shamanism belong here.

B) Pre-arranged premonitory visions (and auditions): these are inner, non-inspirational experiences of a prophetic bearing, which have been prompted in some way or other by the affected persons themselves.

C) Pre-arranged configurations (Sw. *tydor*): human beings themselves build up supernatural experimental situations in which the higher orders of law or finality that determine life are explored, or in which the veil is lifted from various secret matters, such as witchcraft trials and their various tests in order to find out whether or not the accused person is a witch.

Year walk is, as we have seen, definitely an active form of divination centred on spontaneous visionary and auditory experiences, based on a system of preparatory techniques and interpretations. Therefore it can be seen as pre-arranged premonitory visions (2b in the classification above) that have been stimulated by the year walkers themselves.

Popular forms of divination are found outside of the institutional religious context and interact with it at different levels, from conflicting to complementary. Inadequate attention has been given to divination in its own right, independent of institutional religious contexts – that is, to the folk beliefs and their use of divination, and the interaction between practitioners of divination and the general population. Particular forms of divining rely on spontaneous reception of knowledge through intuitive or altered mental states. The use of special techniques and instruments can also lead to acquisition of knowledge (cf. O'Connor 2011). Sometimes special rituals are needed for the technique to be effective, which is the case with year walk. As with any sort of folklore, the details of how this is accomplished may vary. One constant in the records is the importance of time and direction. The ritual was accomplished at midnight or before dawn, and movement had to be performed in certain ways, usually leftwards. The counter-clockwise motion meant going around a house, church, hay-stack, or object a certain number of times. Another aspect, involved how a year walker acquired omens through sensory perception. They are central to all forms of intuitive divination: dreams and visions, auditory sensations, change of taste and smell, inner voices and directives, optical illusions or hallucinatory experiences, heightened and changed emotional, mental and physical states, perceptions of signs and omens, and so on.

Parts of the year walk ritual can be compared with the basic pattern for love divination. Its principles and underlying pattern can be summarised as follows: if someone 1) does something 2) in a certain way 3) at a certain time, 4) he or she will discover his or her future spouse. When it comes to the pattern for year walk, it basically follows the same structure. The outcome might also be grim for both forms of divination, and the consequences that the unpredictable future shows, through signs and omens, might be horrific. In older records, love divination usually clusters around certain important calendar days (Halloween, Midsummer, St Agnes Eve, St Valentine's Day, New Year), and the symbolic power of the particular date is enhanced by the time of day, with midnight usually being most potent. If love divination is performed in the wrong order, or somehow the rules are broken, then it is – just as with year walk – for naught.

Nowadays, it might be hard to grasp the aspects and need for something as exotic as a year walk. This has to do with rapid urbanisation. The village communities have dissolved, and the villages have expanded into rural centres at such a pace that contemporary people cannot apprehend the way in which older generations were bound to the village community and traditions in all aspects of life. People viewed life in a different way and lived in fear of the supernatural: the world abounded with unpredictable events that were frequently explained as being caused by unseen, unpredictable, and supernatural beings and influences; good and ill luck; fate; and so on. We might be on slippery ground if we generalise too much about preindustrial village life, even for an agrarian life that seems as homogenous as Sweden's (Frykman & Löfgren 1980). When it comes to different legends, there is a chance that some of them might have been told as entertainment. Many legends speak of a world and a worldview that is taken seriously, especially in a genre such as belief legends, and that world is not fictional but is very real. People's attitudes towards supernatural experiences were also different from today and did not need explaining in the same way (cf. Virtanen 1992). Supernatural beings existed, and many people believed in them. We have many examples of people in preindustrial Sweden who were put to death by court order because they were believed to have fornicated with beings such as the forest nymph or the neck (Häll 2013). Time and space played significant roles in folklore. It is difficult, perhaps even impossible, at our present state of knowledge, to fully understand or interpret the meaning of many of the different customs and beliefs associated with time, space, boundaries, luck, fate, supernatural forces, and so on. There is plenty of evidence that points to the importance of calendar divination, where a large body of beliefs and customs are based around a particular date or period. The calendar combines the religious, the cultic, and the practical. Year walk can be seen as one of many possible expressions of this: It served a desire to lift the veil of what is hidden and unknown and cross the barriers of space and time.

One final question needs some clarification: is year walk forgotten? I would not hesitate to say yes, as far as the old ritual and practice goes. Appropriately, however, something took place recently in southern Sweden: a small game developing studio in Lund called Simogo decided to base one of its games on a curious ritual that one of its developers had picked up from a popular handbook on Swedish folklore (*Årets högtider* by Ebbe Schön). Inspired by what they could learn of the custom, and with a lot of artistic interpretation, *Year Walk* leapt into the popular imagination worldwide on 21 February 2013. It was released first as an iOS-game and later converted and reworked for PC. This tendency to market folklore and supernatural beings for entertainment serves another purpose: It makes sure that the old narratives and beliefs survive in a new environment. With this article, I hope that the old custom will also receive attention and inspire a scholarly as well as a public audience.

Acknowledgements

I would like to express my gratitude to Bengt af Klintberg, who gave me tips on literature, and to Justin Armstrong who did a first proof reading of my text.

References
Unpublished Literature

E.U. – *Etnologiska undersökningen, Nordiska museet, Stockholm.*
IFGH – *Institutet för folklore vid Göteborgs universitet.*
ULMA – *Dialekt- och folkminnesarkivet, Uppsala.*

Published Literature

Aðalsteinsson J.H. 1978. *Under the Cloak. The Acceptance of Christianity in Iceland with Particular Reference to the Religious Attitudes Prevailing at the Time.* Uppsala: Acta Universitatis Upsaliensis (Studia Ethnologica Upsaliensia, 4).

Arndt, Ernst Moritz. [1807] 1994. *Resa genom Sverige år 1804.* J. M. Stjernstolpe (Transl.). Degeberga: Ultima Thule bokförlag.

Baycroft, T. & D. Hopkin (Eds.). 2012. *Folklore and Nationalism in Europe during the Long Nineteenth Century.* Leiden: Brill (National Cultivation of Culture, 4).

Bergstrand, C-M. 1937. De dödas julotta i västsvensk folktradition. In: *Folkminnen och folktankar*, 24. Göteborg: Västsvenska folkminnesföreningen, pp.118-132.

Bergstrand, C-M. 1939. Årsgången i Västergötland. In: *Folkminnen och folktankar*, 26. Göteborg: Västsvenska folkminnesföreningen, pp. 14-28.

Cameron, E. [2010] 2013. *Enchanted Europe. Superstitions, Reason & Religion, 1250-1750*. Oxford: Oxford University Press.

Celander, H. 1928. *Nordisk jul I. Julen i gammaldags bondesed*. Stockholm: Hugo Gebers förlag.

Christiansen, R.T. [1958] 1992. *The Migratory Legends*. Helsinki: Academia Scieniarum Fennica (Folklore Fellowship Communications, 175).

Davies, O. 2003. *Cunning Folk: Popular Magic in English History*. London: Hambledon Continuum.

Drobin, U. 1983. *Folklore and Comparative Religion*. Stockholm.

Dronke, U. 1997. *The Poetic Edda. Volume II: Mythological Poems*. Oxford: Clarendon Press.

Ellis, B. 2004. *Lucifer Ascending. The Occult in Folklore and Popular Culture*. Lexington: The University Press of Kentucky.

Feilberg, H. F. 1904. *Jul*, vol. I-II. Copenhagen.

Fritzner, J. [1833-1896] 1954. *Ordbog over Det gamle norske Sprog*, vol. I-III. Second, revised edition. Oslo: Tryggve Juul Møller forlag.

Frykman, J. & O. Löfgren. [1980] 1987. *Culture Builders: a Historical Anthropology of Middle-class Life*. A. Crozier (Transl.). New Brunswick: Rutgers University Press.

Gaslander, Petrus. [1772] 1982. *Beskriftning om Svenska Allmogens Sinneslag och Seder, Västbo Härad, Småland*, Stockholm: Bokförlaget Redivia (Suecica Rediviva. A Collection of Facsimile Reprints of Swedish Books, 97).

Hagberg, L. 1937. *När döden gästar. Svenska folkseder och svensk folktro i samband med död och begravning.* Stockholm: Wahlström & Widstrand.

Halvorsen, E. F. & M. Rindal (eds.). 2008. *De eldste østlandske kristenrettene. Tekst etter håndskriftene, med oversettelser.* Oslo: Riksarkivet (Norrøne tekster, 7).

Hultkrantz, Å. 1976. Divinationsformer – en klassifikation. In: *Fataburen. Nordiska museets och Skansens årsbok.* Lund: Nordiska museet, pp. 49–70.

Häll, M. 2013. *Skogsrået, näcken och Djävulen. Erotiska naturväsen och demonisk sexualitet i 1600- och 1700-talens Sverige.* Tallinn: Malört.

Jørgensen, T. 2013. Insiders and Outsiders: Theological 'Landscaping' in early Medieval Provincial Laws in Norway. In: *Sacred Sites and Holy Places. Exploring the Sacralization of Landscape through Time and Space,* S. W. Nordeide & S. Brink (Eds). Turnhout: Brepols (Studies in the Early Middle Ages, 11), pp. 237-251.

af Klintberg, B. 2010. *The Types of the Swedish Folk Legend.* Helsinki: Academia Scieniarum Fennica (Folklore Fellowship Communications, 300).

Lecouteux, C. [1991] 2011.*Phantom Armies of the Night.The Wild Hunt and the Processions of the Undead.*

Lindow, J. 1982. Swedish Legends of Buried Treasure. In: *The Journal of American Folklore* 95 (377), pp. 257-279.

Mitchell, S. A. 2011. *Witchcraft and Magic in the Nordic Middle Ages.* Philadelphia & Oxford: University of Pennsylvania Press.

Odstedt, E. 2004. *Norrländsk folktradition.* Uppteckningar i urval och med kommentarer av Bengt af Klintberg Uppsala: Gustav Adolfs Akademien för svensk folkkultur (Acta Academiae Regiae Gustaci Adolph, 84).

Odstedt, E. 2012 [1943]. Varulven i svensk folktradition. New edition with appendices, P. Faxneld & P. Norström (Eds.). Tallinn: Malört förlag.

O'Connor, K. M. 2011. Divination. In: *Folklore: An Encyclopedia of Beliefs, Customs, Tales, Music, and Art*, 1. K. White & C. McCormick (Eds.). Santa Barbara, Denver & Oxford: ABC-CLIO, pp. 378-390.

Olrik, A.1909. At side paa Høj (oldtidens konger og oldtidens thulir). In: *Danske Studier*, pp. 1-10.

Ó Súilleabháin, S. 1942. *A Handbook of Irish Folklore*. Wexford: The Folklore Society of ireland.

Pape, J. 1946. Studier om kyrkogrimen. In: *Folkkultur. Meddelande från Lunds universitets folkminnesarkiv*, Lund: Gleerup, pp. 11-240.

Rudebeck, Petter. [1700] 1997. *Småländska antiquiteter. Efter ett 300-årigt manuskript av Petter Rudebeck*. G. & G. Liljenroth (Eds.). Lidköping: AMA förlag.

Samplonius, K. 1995. From Veleda to the Völva. Aspects of Female Divination in Germanic Europe. In: *Sanctity and Motherhood. Essays on Holy Mothers in the Middle Ages*. A. Mulder-Bakker (Ed.). New York: Routledge (Garland Medieval Casebooks, 14) pp. 69-100.

Skott, F. 2010. Hilding Celander (1876-1965). In: *Svenska etnologer och folklorister*. Hellspong M. & F. Skott F. (Eds.) Uppsala: Kungl. Gustav Adolfs Akademien (Acta Academiae Regiae Gustavi Adolphi CIX), pp. 69-77.

Strömbäck, D. [1935] 2000. *Sejd och andra studier i nordisk själsuppfattning*. Gertrud Gidlund (Ed.). Södertälje: Gidlunds förlag (Acta Academiae Regiae Gustavi Adolphi, 72)

Tillhagen, CH. [1968] 1980. *Folklig spådomskonst*. Avesta: Fabel.

Virtanen, L. 1992. Have ghosts vanished with industrialism? In: *Folklore Processed in Honour of Lauri Honko on his 60ʰ Birthday*

6ʰ *March 1992.* R. Kvideland et. al. (Eds.) Helsinki: Suomalaisen Kirjallisuuden Seura (Studia Fennica Folkloristica, 1), pp. 225-231.

de Vries, J.1956-57. *Altgermanische Religionsgeschichte* I-II. Second, revised edition.Berlin: Walter de Gruyter & Co.

Wallin, C. 1941. Årsgång och årsgångare i blekinsk folktro och folksed. In: *Blekingeboken. Årsbok.* Karlskrona: Blekinge musei- och hembygsförbunds förlag, pp. 101-136.

Weiser-Aal, L. 1963. Jul. In: *Kulturhistoriskt lexikon för nordisk medeltid,* 8. Malmö: Allhems förlag, pp. 6-14.

Wilby, E. [2005] 2013. *Cunning Folk and Familiar Spirits. Shamanistic Visionary Traditions in Early Modern British Witchcraft and Magic.* Brighton, Chicago & Toronto: Sussex Academic Press.

Chapter 4
Folklore of Manhole Covers: Fears, Hopes and Everyday Magic in Contemporary Sweden

Fredrik Skott
The Institute for Language and Folklore, Gothenburg, Sweden

On the morning of 2 April 2014, someone reported a suspected drunk driver to the police in Linköping. When the police checked the driver, however, they discovered that the she was not in the least intoxicated. Instead, the rickety ride had another explanation: The driver had tried to avoid manhole covers marked with the letter A. The story quickly spread all over Sweden via the news agency TT. Judging from comments on social media, some people wondered what it was all about, while others recognized themselves in the narrative. It is obvious that knowledge of the danger posed by the A-covers differs from generation to generation in contemporary Sweden.

Like most people of my age, I remember the manhole covers from my own childhood in Säffle, a small city in the province of Värmland. In the 1980s it was common knowledge among my friends that manhole covers marked with an A (so called *A-brunnar*, in English: A-covers) meant bad luck, whereas you had good luck if you walked on K-covers. Fortunately, protective rituals existed for those who accidentally stepped on or cycled over an A-cover.

The folklore of manhole covers is one example of what is often called 'superstition'. Alan Dundes (1961: 28; cf. Valk 2008: 14) has defined the term as "traditional expressions of one or more conditions and one or more results with some of the conditions, signs and other causes." In the book *Emergence of Folklore in Everyday Life*, Kenneth Pimple (1995: 96; cf. Kukharenko 2008: 57) emphasizes that superstition is beliefs "usually about luck and concerned with the successful completion of a specific task, often associated with ritual behaviors." In Swedish, however, terms like superstition (*skrock* or *vidskepelse*) are heavily loaded with (negative) values. In this context, I therefore use "everyday magic" for corresponding beliefs (cf. Valk 2008).

It is mainly children and young people who take an active part in the tradition concerning manhole covers. For the vast majority, the notions and rituals are somewhere in the borderland between playfulness and seriousness. The different meanings of the letters on the manhole covers should be regarded as an expression of young people's creativity, but to some extent the changes of the narratives can also be understood as a form of a 'social barometer'. As the folklorist Ulf Palmenfelt (2008: 12) has stated, folklore can be understood as tools for formulating, communicating, comparing, consolidating, and questioning values. With this article, I not only want to discuss the notions of manhole covers as examples of everyday magic in Sweden but also show how the tradition and its change reflects both fears and hopes of young people in 20th- and 21st-Century Sweden. The cited texts are translated from Swedish by me.

Narratives about manhole covers
The day after the TT article about the unsteady car drive in Linköping, I made an appeal on the website of the Institute for Language and Folklore for narratives about manhole covers and published a web questionnaire, put together in great haste:

Have you heard what the letters on the manhole covers are supposed to represent or be abbreviations of? Tell us. Should one avoid stepping on some covers? Why? Could you protect yourself if you accidentally step on a 'bad/dangerous' cover? Are there any 'good' covers – which? Please specify the place and time you tell about (e.g. Säffle in the 1980s or Stockholm in the 1950s). Do you avoid stepping on some covers? Tell us. Do you know where the tradition comes from or how old it is? Are there similar traditions in other countries? (http://www.sprakochfolkminnen.se/ga-pa-gatubrunnar)

The appeal had a major impact. After a link to the web questionnaire was published on Facebook, information about the appeal spread quickly. Several Swedish newspapers wrote about the web questionnaire, and a number of radio stations mentioned the subject. In just over a week, nearly 400 people sent their narratives about manhole covers to the Institute. The material is now a part of the collections at the Department of Dialectology, Onomastics and Folklore Research in Göteborg (DAGF 1612).

Certainly, many of the adults that responded to the web questionnaire still avoid stepping on A-covers, out of habit or just to be on the safe side, but it is obvious that it is mainly a tradition among children and young people. Most respondents tell about the notions and rituals as memories of their childhood, as something that characterized life during parts of their school time. It is primarily women who responded to the web questionnaire; only about 15% of those answering were men. The narratives themselves also reveal that the ideas about the different meanings of the covers are, and always have been, primarily spread among young women. For example, a woman born in 1974 in Salem writes: "I think this thing with the covers was most common among the girls." And a few years younger man in Gammelstad notes: "It was nothing I believed in, but I remember that it was popular among the girls at that time, and for a while it spread like wildfire among the schools in the town." The transmission of the tradition seems mainly to take place horizontally: The notions exist and are spread most in interaction between young people (cf. af Klintberg 2007a: 80).

As with many other forms of folklore, it is difficult to prove exactly how and when the tradition originated. The earliest records of 'unlucky' manhole covers are from Göteborg in the late 1940s and early 1950s. From the mid-1950s, there are also records from Stockholm, and during the following decade, the tradition seems to have appeared in numerous Swedish cities, such as Eskilstuna, Hallsberg, Karlskrona, Karlstad, Kristianstad, Linköping, Malmö, Sala, Skellefteå, Uddevalla, and Uppsala. In the 1970s, the notions seem to have spread all over Sweden. It is easy to explain that it is a tradition that mainly exists in cities, as there are few manhole covers in rural areas.

The meaning of the letters on the manhole covers varies, both in folklore and 'in reality'. In an interview, one of those responsible for the drainage and piping systems in Göteborg, says that the 'real' meaning of the letters may differ between municipalities and over time. Sometimes the letters are abbreviations for those producing the covers (A for Alvesta foundry and K for Karlstad foundry), but just as often the letters reflect the function. Thus A means *Avlopp* (Drains), K stands for a *Kombinerad* (Combined) pipe for waste water and surface water, V for *Ventil* (Valve), FV for *Fjärrvärme* (District heating), *etc.*

Like other forms of folklore, the notions and rituals about manhole covers are both individual and collective; the tradition has fixed frames, but the elements vary across time and place and to some extent even from person to person. However, A-covers are frequently associated with bad luck and K-covers with luck, especially with love. But other meanings can also be attached to the letters. In the following, I will describe and discuss both how the interpretation of the letters reflects young people's hopes and fears, and how the tradition can be understood as a method to manage and explain the unexplainable in the practitioners' lives and environment.

From corporal punishment to AIDS
As noted, it is generally assumed that it brings bad luck to step on an A-cover. However, more than half of those responding to the web questionnaire also write about more specific meanings: how you are supposed to get bad luck or what will happen if you accidentally touch a manhole cover marked with the letter A.

Common in the 1960s, as well as in the 2010s, is that the letter A on the manhole covers is repeatedly interpreted as *Avbruten kärlek* (Interrupted love) or *Aldrig kärlek* (Never love, 75 – the numbers indicate the number of respondents that mention the interpretation). A man born in 1974 in Skurup remembers: "If you had a girlfriend/ boyfriend, he or she would break it off if you stepped on an A-cover." A similar explanation is given by a woman born in 1975 in Forsa: "If you are single, you would not get together with the person you dream about. And if you are in a relationship, it will end." Most often A-covers were simply avoided by walking around or jumping over them, but in some cases the manhole covers could be used to end an awkward relationship. "A close friend of mine used the manhole covers when she underwent a difficult separation. She sought out the A-covers as they meant 'interrupted love', and that was what she wanted – that her love for her ex-boyfriend would disappear. This was in Stockholm at the end of the 1990s" (woman, b. 1967).

Although *Avbruten kärlek* (Interrupted love) is the most common explanation for the A on the covers, there are also a number of other meanings. From the 1950s to the 1970s, the letter was sometimes supposed to mean *Avund/Avundsjuka* (Envy/Jealousy,

24). This meant that by stepping on an A-cover you would be jealous or be affected by another person's envy (cf. Strömbäck 1989:19–24). From the city of Malmö, a woman born in 1981 writes: "I think I was about thirteen years old when a friend told me that you should not step on A-covers because A stands for *Avundsjuka* (Jealousy) and if you walk on A-covers bad things could happen in your life as you 'open up' for other people's dark thoughts and envy." *Avsky* (Loathing, 13) and *Avgrund* (Abyss, 9) are other meanings that existed during the same period. Additional meanings from the 1950s, 1960s, and 1970s are *Akta/Akta dig* (Watch out, 3), *Arbetslös/Avskedad* (Unemployed/Fired, 3), *Aga* (Corporal punishment, 2), and *Avsked* (Farewell, 2).

Besides the meanings mentioned above, the A-covers were also interpreted in new ways during the 1980s and 1990s: *Analsex* (Anal sex, 12), *Apa/Apskaft* (Monkey/Monkeyhead, 10), *Alkholist/ Alkoholism* (Alcoholic/Alcoholism, 7), *Analklåda/Analproblem* (Anal itching/Anal problems, 5), Anorexia (5), *Abort* (Abortion, 4), and AIDS (4) are among the interpretations that are mentioned in the answers to the web questionnaire. Other examples from the late 20th Century are *Allvar/Allvarlig* (Seriousness/Serious, 3), *Avfall* (Garbage, 2), Acne (1), Aliens come and get you (1), Amalgam (1), Anaconda (1), Anarchy (1), *Andar* (Spirits, 1), Apathy (1), Asocial (1), Atomic bomb (1), and *Avrättning* (Execution, 1). The major reason why some of the meanings above became widespread is Lukas Moodysson's movie *Fucking Åmål* (English title: *Show Me Love*) from 1998. In Sweden, nearly a million people saw the film, and for many it nearly defines the 1990s. Briefly, the movie is about the two teenage girls, Agnes and Elin, about friendship, love, sexuality, everyday life in a small town in western Sweden, and the longing to get away from it. In one of the most talked-about scenes, Elin is warned by her older sister Jessica not to stand on an A-cover:

JESSICA: Don't stand there!

Elin looks blankly at Jessica.

ELIN: What?

JESSICA: A-cover.

Elin is in fact standing with one foot on a manhole cover with the letter A on.

ELIN: Grow up!

JESSICA: Acne. Abortion. *Arbetslöshet* (Unemployment). Alcoholic. Anorexia.

ELIN: Do you still go to kindergarten?

JESSICA: Anal sex. Asthma. AIDS.

Jessica gets up on another manhole cover, one metre in front of Elin.

ELIN: But hey, are you completely stupid? You are standing on a cover yourself!

JESSICA: But this is a K-cover.

ELIN: But it is only you that believe that K means *Kärlek* (love). Do you know what it really means? It means *Kräkas* (Vomit)!

JESSICA: Move now.

ELIN: *Kondylom* (Condyloma). And Cancer.

JESSICA: Oh my God, I get so irritated! Must you always do the opposite?

Elin starts demonstratively to stomp and jump on the A-cover.

ELIN: Ok, we're testing. I do like this: Abortion! *Arbetslös* (Unemployed)! Anal sex!

Elin stops

ELIN: No .... I feel nothing. No anal sex.

JESSICA: You're not normal.

Elin walks away. (Moodysson 1998)

Although many of the interpretations existed before *Fucking Åmål*, the impact the film had on the tradition cannot be underestimated.

Many who answered the web questionnaire state how much they were affected by the film and how they identified with its leading characters. A dozen respondents point out that the movie in various ways directly contributed to spreading and changing notions about the different manhole covers. For example, one woman born in 1981 in Göteborg writes: "As a teenager the meanings of the manhole covers developed as one can see in *Fucking Åmål*."

The meaning of the A-covers thus varies, both over time and sometimes dependent of the practitioner's age. Something that has hardly changed, however, is the rituals used to neutralize bad luck when accidentally stepping on an A-cover. In a few answers to the web questionnaire, it is mentioned that in such cases you should quickly locate and step on a 'good' cover. Most frequently mentioned, however, is that the misfortune could be neutralized if someone patted you on your back three times. A woman raised in Skattkärr in the province of Värmland in the 1980s writes: "A stands for *Avbruten kärlek* (Interrupted love). You should not step on such a cover, but if you should happen to step on it, someone should pat you on your back three times. This will prevent it. You can pat yourself three times on your back too, but it may not be as good." From Gävle in the 1980s, another woman recalls: "If you were walking and pushing a pram with your younger brother or sister in, you had to clap both the children and the pram. It could be a lot of claps if you had a lot of things in the pram that you cared about. I remember that we once clapped a football for safety's sake (it is unclear what we thought would happen to it)."

K-covers and love
In contrast to A-covers, which are said to be 'bad', K-covers are usually described as 'good' or 'lucky' covers. Another difference is that there are many fewer variations when it comes to K-covers.

Most of those who have responded to the web questionnaire write that K stands for *Kärlek* (Love): By stepping on a K-cover you would be able to win or keep someone's love. "The K-covers ... stand for *Kärlek* (Love) and luck and I/we searched for them and tried to use their power!" a woman born in 1965 in Mölndal writes. From Göteborg in the early 1970s, a woman remembers: "If we were in love with someone we had an awfully tough job to ensure that we stepped on every K-cover on our way to or from school." Even in the 1990s, the K-covers were exclusively described as love-covers: "One should jump on them and think of one person – then he/she would fall in love with you. And how we jumped! We looked up which routes through the residential neighbourhood garnered the most covers, and sometimes ran long detours to get the opportunity to 'pick' those extra three covers that might make the big difference" (woman, b. 1988, Mölndal). It is often reported that it was enough to step on a K-cover, but sometimes more complicated rituals were necessary to arouse someone's love:

A cover with a K on it means *Kärlek* (Love), and you SHOULD step on it. Ideally you should stand on the cover a few seconds, or walk very slowly across it, and quietly whisper the name of the person you are in love with to make it come true that the person will love you (woman, b. 1981, Kungälv).

K-cover: You should step on it, while saying 'K-cover, luck in *Kärlek* (Love).' Then you should have a better chance of winning the person you were thinking of. But it only worked for one person at a time, so for two persons it was 'first come, first serve', and then it took a time of uncertain length before the power of the cover was back again (woman, b. 1976, Stockholm).

In order to 'boost the effect' on luck in *Kärlek* (Love) at K, a friend and I kissed the K-cover while we were thinking of a boy who we found interesting at the time. It was somewhat embarrassing as he just cycled past us when we lay there … nor did it work (woman, b. 1969, Emmaboda).

Even if K-covers were generally considered to be 'lucky' covers, some of those responding to the web questionnaire write that they avoided them when they were younger. A man born in 1975 in Västerås remembers: "[Love] was embarrassing when one was so young." And a girl born in 2005 in Uppsala writes: "The love cover is the one with a K on it. If you step on that you fell in love for two years, you can fall in love with anyone. It is bad."

Get friends, become beautiful, or end up in jail
From the 1960s and onwards, different meanings have also been linked to other kinds of manhole covers, especially V- (*Ventil*, Valve), FV- (*Fjärrvärme*, District heating), and *Telefon*-covers (Telephone) as well as road drains.

Most often it is believed to be good or lucky to step on a V-cover. The letter V was interpreted as *Vänner/Vänskap* (Friends/Friendship, 55), but from the 1980s onwards it could also mean *Vacker* (Beautiful, 11) or *Vinst/Vinner* (Prize/Winner, 8). Other interpretations that are mentioned in the answers to the web questionnaire are *Våldtäkt* (Rape, 3), *Vanskapt* (Malformed, 1), *Vampyr* (Vampire, 1), *Vigsel* (Wedding, 1), and *Visdom* (Wisdom, 1). "V-covers were friendship covers. You were supposed to hold your best friend by the hand and jump on the covers, and then that friendship would last forever," writes a woman born in 1988 in Mölndal. From Växjö in the 1990s, another woman remembers: "There was a V-cover on my way home that I always tried to step on when I was at high school. I had no good friends and wanted so much to have friends" (woman, b. 1986, Växjö).

FV-covers were sometimes associated with *Fara väntar* (Danger awaits, 4), *Flickvän* (Girlfriend, 2), *Förlovad* (Engaged, 1), *Farlig vänskap* (Dangerous friendship, 1), or *Förfärligt vacker* (Terribly beautiful, 1). The meanings of the road drains were always negative. In about twenty narratives, road drains (with 'bars') are interpreted as *Fängelse* (Jail), meaning that a person who stepped on them or that person's parents would end up in jail. To walk on a cover that says *Tele* (Telephone) or *Rikstele* (National telephone) was sometimes interpreted to mean that you would soon get a phone call or a very high phone bill.

Rituals, hopes, and fears
As noted above, stepping on or avoiding manhole covers should partly be understood as a game. A woman in Göteborg born in 1989 says: "It was ... something that made the walk or a school trip a little bit more fun." However, many of those answering the web questionnaire also describe how they took the narratives about different manhole covers very seriously when they were young, how they persistently avoided every A-cover, while looking for and trying to step on K-covers.

Like other forms of everyday magic, the rituals regarding manhole covers concern areas in the practitioners' lives that engage them, are perceived as important, and at the same time are 'unsafe' and hard to control (Palmenfelt 2008: 8; cf. Tucker 2012: 396–398). "Superstition is a way of managing irrationality in our world," as Utz Jeggle and John Bendix (2003: 82) put it. Robert Georges and Michel Jones (1995: 96) stress that 'superstition' mostly relates to events or conditions "over which human beings have no control and which they regard and interpret."

Friendship and love are central themes of rituals related to manhole covers. Both emotional themes occupy large parts of our time and are a source of both joy and concern, perhaps even more so during adolescence. The website umo.se, "a youth-friendly clinic online," expresses it in the following manner: "One friendship can feel cosy and safe, and another may feel tough and demanding. For some, it is a matter of course to have buddies, while others do not think they have any friends. Love may be beautiful and fun, but also painful with feelings like jealousy and anxiety. Being together with someone could be the thing you crave most of all, or you can most of all long to break up." The rituals related to manhole covers can at least partly be understood as methods of coping and to some extent controlling these areas. For example, by stepping on certain manhole covers, you can increase the possibility of getting together with the one you love or acquiring more friends.

But just as often, the manhole covers are used to consolidate existing love relations and friendships. A woman born in the middle of the 1970s in Hägersten writes: "V meant *Vänner* (Friends). Sometimes you stepped on it together with you friends and laughed about it. As if confirming the friendship." Some of those responding to the web questionnaire also remembered that couples could stand together on a K-cover, probably as a method both to manifest and to maintain the love for each other (cf. Kättström Höök 2012: 93). As with other forms of folklore, the rituals can be understood as methods of *formulating, communicating*, and not least *comparing* feelings (Palmenfelt 2008: 8). Several respondents, for instance, write that they used to compete with others. As part of the ritual, the one that first came to the manhole cover would say, or even better call out, the name of the person she was secretly in love with.

In the mid-70s, in Uppsala, we avoided A-covers as they meant a lot of bad luck. On the other hand, K-covers meant *KÄRLEK* (love) and when we were about 10 years old we competed over who first got to jump on the manhole cover and call out a name of a person we were in love with. If you were lucky enough to come to the cover first, you had to spit on it 3 times … it meant that no one could call out the same name until the spittle had dried. A few years later, it was enough to bike over a K-cover and think of the person you were in love with (woman, b. 1965, Uppsala).

That the letters on the manhole covers sometimes were given specific meanings can, as stated, be seen as a rash of young people's creativity, but the associations also reflect widespread fears during the 19th and 20th Centuries (cf. af Klintberg 2007b: 114–128; Stattin 1990; Virtanen 1976: 257–258). Besides interrupted love and betrayal by friends, notions about manhole covers reflect fears of addiction (alcoholism), violence (corporal punishment, rape), bullying (being called a monkey), dentists (amalgam), and suffering accidents or diseases (AIDS, acne, anorexia, asthma, etc.). Other meanings reflect concerns about finances (unemployment, high telephone bills) or losing someone you care about (farewell). The notions about street drains are another clear example of how the manhole covers reflect young people's fears. "If you accidentally stepped on these bars, it meant that you would end up in prison, or that you would be kidnapped and locked in," writes a woman born in Malmö in 1976. "This made all of us kids scared," another respondent says.

The folklore of manhole covers is to some extent time-bound. For example, the A-covers were interpreted as *Arbetslöshet/Avskedad* (Unemployment/Fired) during the 1970s, a topic connected to the recession that hit the Western world during that decade. And it is hardly a coincidence that interpretations such as Anorexia, AIDS, and Atomic Bomb arose during the 1980s and 1990s. The increasing sexualisation of society in the late 1900s has also affected the tradition. This applies to the A-covers but to some extent also to the K-covers. A woman born in 1991 in Vänersborg writes: "Most of the later parts of the time in high school were characterized by love, relationships, and sex, which were reflected in virtually everything; even the manhole covers." A man from Nyköping, born in 1983, says: "I also remember how the K-covers during school time all of a sudden got sexual interpretations, that is, if a boy and a girl together walked over a K-cover, it meant that they would, well….."

Love magic of today?
As I have stated, the tradition concerning A- and K-covers seems to have originated in Sweden. The tradition appears to have been largely unknown in Denmark, Norway, and Finland, at least before the film *Fucking Åmål*. However, similar notions and rituals seem to exist in Great Britain. In his book *Penguin Guide to the Superstitions of Britain and Ireland*, Stephen Roud (2003: 353-354) mentions that it is bad luck to cross three manhole covers in a row. I called for more narratives about manhole covers in *FLS News*, the newsletter of the Folklore Society. A teacher who had been documenting folklore among children in a school in Coventry in the 1990s wrote:

> Walking over single manhole covers was unlucky, double manhole covers lucky and treble manhole covers VERY unlucky. One pupil believed if you walked over a treble cover you had to walk backwards over it again (returning to the beginning as it were) and then avoid it the next time. Another pupil claimed that to get rid of the bad luck you had to spit on the last cover (of the three) and yet another said you had to cross the road and not return to your original route until you had walked over a double one (letter from Cathy Gould, 21 May 2014).

A colleague from Russia also informed me that similar notions are common among children in Siberia. At least in the Tyumen district, stepping on a manhole cover is assumed to bring bad luck in general or, more specifically, mean that your mother will die. If you accidentally step on a cover, you can neutralize the bad luck by taking three steps crouching (letter from Elena Yugay, 17 April 2014; cf. Bayduzh 2012). Notions linked to manhole covers thus also exist in other countries, but it seems as if the rituals' connection with love is only found in Sweden.

The narratives and notions about A- and K-covers are a relatively new phenomenon. However, hopes of managing, not to mention controlling, love are nothing new. Already in Swedish collections of superstitions from the 17th, 18th, and 19th Centuries, several methods can be found for arousing or assuaging love. For example, in *Samling av widskeppelser* from the 18th Century, Johan J. Törner writes "with a sewing needle, which has been used to sew on corpses, you can make a person in love with you, if you put the needle in their clothes" (Wikman 1946: 88). In Leonhard Fredrik Rääf's collection *Svenska skrock och signerier* from the 19th Century, there are about 50 different forms of love magic, for example: "put 3 drops of blood, taken from under the left wing of a bat, on a handkerchief, which you then rub gently on the mouth of a girl to arouse her love" (Wikman 1957: 266; cf. Gasslander 1982; Tillhagen 1959; Wallensteen 1899). In the Swedish folklore archives, there are thousands of records about similar rituals (cf. Schön 1996). It is possible to understand the rituals concerning A- and K-covers as a modern form of love magic, a simpler and contemporary equivalent of the peasant society's often rather complicated rituals with the same purpose. Thus, the rituals have changed, but the notions about manhole covers show that young people are still in need of 'magic' rituals to explain and, more or less seriously, try to control the search for love in their lives.

[107]

As I have mentioned, the notions of manhole covers are usually somewhere in the borderland between playfulness and seriousness (cf. Kvideland 1976: 248). Probably the same applies to similar rituals of older times. It is likely that these kinds of traditions have always primarily been spread among young people. At least several of those responding to the web questionnaire have described the tradition as something that they used to believe in or practised when young. However, the answers also reveal that the driver in Linköping who was mentioned at the beginning of the article is far from the only adult who avoids A-covers. Actually, over one-fifth of the 400 respondents write that as adults, they are reluctant to step on unlucky manhole covers. For example, a woman born in 1967 in Skara says: "Strangely, this is still in me. In front of a cash-dispenser in Skara there is an A-cover! It is a bit tricky not to touch the cover when you collect the money." Many stress that they avoid the covers for safety's sake and often surreptitiously. For example, a woman in Norrtälje, born in 1991, writes: "If I walk alone, I walk in a zigzag pattern to avoid the A-covers." Another narrative, significant in this context, was written by a nearly fifty-year-old woman in Ludvika: "Even to this day, I make little detours, skip and hop or take abnormally long/short steps to avoid stepping on any A-covers. Hope no-one notices ;)"

References
Unprinted sources in the author's possession
Unprinted folklore records: The Institute for Language and Folklore: The Department of Dialectology, Onomastics and Folklore Resarch in Gothenburg (DAGF 1612).
Letter from Cathy Gold, 21 May 2014.
Letter from Elena Yugay, 17 April 2014.

Printed sources

Bayduzh, M. 2012. The transformation of the traditional ideas about the supernatural in an urban environment. The experience of collecting and organizing of material. In: *Folklore and Cultural Anthropology Today. Abstracts and Materials International School-Conference*. A. Arkhipova et al. (Eds.) Moscow, pp. 255–261.

Dundes, A. 1961. Brown County Superstitions. The Structure of Superstition. In: *Midwest Folklore* 11 (1), pp. 25–56.

FLS News. The Newsletter of the Folklore Society 73 (June 2014).

Gasslander, P. 1982. *Beskrifning om Svenska Allmogens Sinnelag och Seder, Västbo Härad, Småland*. Stockholm.

Georges, R. & J. Michael (Eds.). 1995. *Folkloristics. An Introduction*. Bloomington.

Henriksson, B. 2007.*"Var trogen i allt". Den goda kvinnan som konstruktion i svenska och finlandssvenska minnesböcker 1800–1980*. Åbo.

Jeggle, U. & J. Bendix. 2003. A Lost Track. On the Unconscious in Folklore. In: *Journal of Folklore Research* 40 (1), pp. 73–94.

af Klintberg, B. 2007a: *Folkminnen*. Stockholm.

af Klintberg, B. 2007b: "Svarta Madame, kom fram!" In: *Vår tids folkkultur*. B. af Klintberg & U. Palmenfelt (Eds.) Stockholm, pp. 114–128.

Kukharenko, S. 2008. Negotiating Magic. Ukrainian Wedding Traditions and Their Persistence in Canada. In: *Canadian Contributions to the XIV International Congress of Slavists, Ohrid, Macedonia, 2008*, pp. 55–74.

Kvideland, R. 1976. Barnetru. Ein faktor i den kulturelle innlæringsprosessen. In: *Fataburen*, pp. 233–254.

Kättström Höök, L. 2012. Kärlekslås – en ritual för evig kärlek. In: *Fataburen*, pp. 93–111.

Moodysson, L. 1998. *Fucking Åmål Manuskript*. Stockholm.

Palmenfelt, U. 2008. Inledning. In: *Vår tids folkkultur.* B. af Klintberg & U. Palmenfelt (Eds.). Stockholm, pp. 7–13.

Pimple, K. 1990. Folk Beliefs. In: *The Emergence of Folklore in Everyday Life. A Fieldguide and Sourcebook.* G. H. Schoemaker (Ed.). Bloomington, pp. 51–58.

Roud, S. 2003. *The Penguin Guide to the Superstitions of Britain and Ireland.* London: Penguin.

Schön, E. 1996. *Älskogens magi. Folktro om kärlek och lusta.* Stockholm.

Stattin, J. 1990. *Från gastkramning till gatuvåld. En etnologisk studie av svenska rädslor.* Stockholm.

Strömbäck, D. 1989: *Den osynliga närvaron. Studier i folktro och folkdikt.* Hedemora.

Tillhagen, CH. 1959. Bruk i Tjust. Antecknadt 1818 och följande utur hvardagslifvet af E. Havton. In: *Tjustbygdens Kulturhistoriska förenings årsbok,* pp. 5–48.

Tucker, E. 2012. Changing Concepts of Childhood. Children's Folklore Scholarship since the Late Nineteenth Century. In: *Journal of American Folklore* 498, pp. 389–410.

Valk, Ü. 2008: Superstition in Estonian Folklore. From Official Category to Vernacular Concept. In: *Folklore* 119 (1), pp. 14–28.

Virtanen, L. 1976: Lagom lycka är bäst. Magiska föreställningar i dag. In: *Fataburen,* pp. 255–268.

Wikman, K. Rob. V. 1946: *Johan J. Törners samling af widskeppelser.* Uppsala (Skrifter utgivna av Kungl. Gustav Adolfs Akademien, 15).

Wikman, K. Rob. V. 1957: *Svenska skrock och signerier samlade av Leonhard Fredrik Rääf.* Stockholm (Kungl. Vitterhets Historie och Antikvitets Akademiens handlingar. Filologisk-filosofiska serien, 4).

Wallensteen, J. P. 1899: *Vidskepelser, vantro och huskurer i Danderyd och Lidingö i slutet af 1700-talet.* Stockholm (Bidrag till vår odlings häfder, 7).

Chapter 5
Chicken Skin Stories: Folk Belief in Contemporary Hawai'i

Kirsten Møllegaard
University of Hawai'i at Hilo

"We are the ones who speak the stories, our connections."
Ku'ulei Keakealani, Native Hawaiian educator

Introduction: Chicken skin stories
In the spring of 1955, sugarcane field workers and residents of the district of Puna on the island of Hawai'i noticed volcanic fumes amidst sudden fissures in the ground and an increasing number of shallow earthquakes. Soon Kīlauea volcano erupted, sending two lava flows down the slopes towards Puna. The Hawai'i National Guard evacuated the area, and Gordon Morse, a reporter for the *Honolulu Advertiser*, accompanied the manager of the Puna Sugar Company, a scientist, and a pilot on a small plane to inspect the damage done to the cane fields. They landed on an abandoned cinder road. Suddenly they "came upon a Lady sitting at the edge of a sugar field" (Carroll 1997: 4). Morse describes the woman as young, attractive, and graceful, with long black hair down to the middle of her back, barefoot, wearing a red *mu'umu'u* (long loose dress). At first the woman greeted them politely and smiled, but when the men insisted that she must leave the area, she stopped smiling and said, "I follow my own laws" (Carroll 1997: 5). Morse noted that by now her eyes looked like "glowing coals" (1997: 5). Uneasy and perplexed, the men discussed what to do about her.

When they turned around to approach her, she was gone. Morse is convinced she was Pele, the volcano goddess.

Chicken skin tales like Morse's encounter with the volcano goddess Pele exemplify what Homi Bhabha in the context of postcolonial studies refers to as cultural anxiety, and Jacques Derrida in the context of history and lived experience refers to as hauntology. What Morse and his three male companions faced was more than a phantom of an alluring, divine woman: It was the eruptive and creative power of the volcanic landscape itself, a powerful specter of Hawaiian myth and legend. Although Morse, a Caucasian who had settled in Hawai'i, attempted to rationalize the experience, he felt in the end compelled to admit that the mysterious disappearing woman could only have been Pele, thus situating his narrative within the long tradition of Hawaiian chicken skin tales and Pele sightings at the time of volcanic eruptions.

In Hawai'i Creole English (HCE) 'chicken skin' means "to get goose bumps on your skin wen you scared" (Tonouchi 2005: 17). Although the HCE term "chicken skin stories" has been popularized and mainstreamed by Glen Grant, author and folklorist, whose popular *Chicken Skin* book series and radio show featured local Hawaiian ghost lore, folklorists will recognize such oral narratives as contemporary, or urban, legends. Contemporary legends are told in multiple versions. Their "settings are realistic and familiar," and they typically feature ordinary people's encounters with the supernatural or unexplainable (Brunvand 1999: 19). They often focus on deep-rooted cultural values and tensions and are communicated through multiple types of media, sometimes as eyewitness narratives, but frequently told second or third-hand by a friend of a friend (Brunvand 1999: 19). Diana E. Goldstein (2004: 28) summarizes:

They are told as true, factual, or plausible and therefore assume a level of authority; they provoke dialogue about the narrative events, their interpretation, and their plausibility; they both articulate and influence beliefs and attitudes towards the subject matter; and they have the capability of affecting the actions and behavior of the listening audience.

Jan Brunvand declares, "In short, [contemporary legends] are just too darn *good* – that is, polished, balanced, focused, and neat – to be true" (1999: 19; original emphasis). However, trying to establish veracity in contemporary legends distracts from a deeper and socially more relevant concern, namely what their cultural function is. What do such stories say about people's connection to the place they live and their lived experience of everyday culture? Which messages and cultural values are embedded in contemporary legends? The core question is not whether such narratives literally are true (although they to a large degree actually are told *as* true, or at least as *somewhat* true). The central point for this paper is to examine their function as catalysts of cultural values and social anxieties, a point which is of significant importance in a multiethnic island community like Hawai'i, where the historical context of colonialism and non-indigenous settlers have rendered indigenous Hawaiians a minority in their own homeland. Yet, despite the social and economic marginalization of Hawaiians in contemporary Hawai'i, chicken skin stories reinforce traditional Hawaiian cultural values no matter the narrators' own ethnic backgrounds.

From the broader cultural perspective of postcolonial studies, chicken skin tales constitute a tradition of narrative resistance to the western worldviews that have been imposed on Hawaiians and non-Europeans settlers during colonization. In regard to how oral narratives function as tradition, Henry Glassie (1995: 395) argues, "tradition is the creation of the future out of the past." He continues, "Folk and lore link people and expression in a functional circle. Epic and nation, myth and society, custom and community – all conjoin communications and groups. The group exists because its members create communications that call it together and bring it to order. Communications exist because people acting together, telling tales at the hearth, or sending signals through computerized networks develop significant forms that function at once *as signs of identity and forces of cohesion*" (Glassie, 1995: 400; emphasis added).

Chicken skin stories can be viewed as such signposts "of identity and forces of cohesion" among Hawai'i's multiethnic population because of the haunted cultural spaces of pre-colonial Hawai'i that they evoke. The emphasis in chicken skin stories on a powerful spectral and spiritual presence incorporates indigenous Hawaiian cultural traditions and values such as *kapu* (taboo), *mana* (sacred power), *aloha 'aina* (loving and respecting the land), and *malama ka 'aina* (caring for the land). Chicken skin stories sharply deviate from the tourist industry's trivialization, exotification, and emasculation of the people of Hawai'i through powerful male and female specters that signify shared identity and forces of centripetal cultural cohesion.

Methodology and interpretative framework: Historical and cultural contexts
This paper reflects an ongoing folklore project in which students in introductory myth and folklore classes at the University of Hawai'i at Hilo collect contemporary legends and ghost lore associated with specific geographical places on the island of Hawai'i. Fifteen to twenty students per class per semester engage in collecting contemporary legends by each interviewing four to five individuals within a folk group of their own choice, who are asked to tell them about encounters in specific places with the supernatural that they themselves have had, or that people they know have had. Despite the limited number of participants, the results are promising and

[116]

warrant further collection. If the number of interviews is somewhat limited, the geographical perimeter for the oral narratives is wide. The island of Hawai'i is larger than all the other Hawaiian Islands combined and features an extremely varied geography ranging from volcanoes, lava deserts, and mountains to rain forests, pasture land, and verdant valleys. The stories discussed in this paper take place on the roadways between or around the mountains, in coastal valleys, and in areas frequently affected by lava flows from Kīlauea volcano.

Employing the methodology for collecting oral narratives outlined in Donna M. DeBlasio *et al*.'s *Catching Stories: A Practical Guide to Oral History* (2009), students record and transcribe stories told as true in their own folk groups (other students, family, colleagues, sports teams, church communities, and so on). I then corroborate the collected material with print sources, typically (but not always) finding close or very close similarity in narrative structure and content between older print versions and the oral stories collected by the students. The reason for comparing the collected stories with print versions is not to try to establish veracity, but to track the similarity (and hence the narrative tradition) between the oral narratives and the more structured, polished versions found in sources spanning from popular fiction to books on mythology and Hawaiian culture. As folklorist Linda Dégh (2001: 26) observes, "what we collect today uniquely mirrors the ideas of our time." In other words, corroborating the collected stories with print sources establishes important cultural contexts and narrative traditions, but the main focus for interpreting what these stories mean within a multiethnic island community is the cultural values they express. Gillian Bennett and Paul Smith argue that contemporary legends are "believed by the community which transmits them because they resonate with their life circumstances and address their social and/or moral causes" (1996: xxiv). Bengt af Klintberg (1986), Jan Harold Brunvand (1981;

1999), Véronique Campion-Vincent (2005), and other folklorists have noted that contemporary legends typically focus on themes relating to xenophobia (fear of outsiders and strangers); conspiracy theories (evil elites and nefarious schemes);money matters; sexual transgressions (marital infidelity and excessive sexuality); bodily harm (murder, rape, dismemberment, and organ theft); public humiliation (shame); humorous coincidences (comic relief); and creepy encounters with the supernatural. While chicken skin stories may contain some of these themes from western culture, their thematic concerns are overwhelmingly with non-western phenomena like *kapu* (taboo), *mana* (sacred power), *aloha 'aina* (loving and respecting the land), and *malama ka 'aina* (caring for the land). This suggests that the narrators, regardless of their own ethnic backgrounds, acknowledge Hawaiian cultural values and show awareness of a cultural paradigm adverse to, and hence resisting, the westernization of Hawai'i. Morse's encounter with the volcano goddess Pele, who follows "her own laws," may be interpreted as voicing resistance to western dominance, which is here seen as gendered and technocratic: non-native men representing science, money, technology, and historiography arrive by plane and tell a barefoot native woman to leave the land. Undoubtedly Morse did not intend his account to be read this way, but when the story is seen as a subtext to political efforts to reestablish Hawaiian sovereignty, the men's failed attempt to order Pele out of the district of Puna, her homeland, implies a symbolic vindication for native rights to land and sovereignty.

Regarding the interpretation of the collected narratives, it cannot be ignored that the postcolonial revitalization of the Hawaiian language and cultural traditions that were suppressed during Western colonization of Hawai'i plays a significant role in the emphasis on Hawaiian cultural values in these informal, oral narratives. However, my interpretation and contextualization of the collected narratives do not attempt to establish a hierarchy of cultural authenticity, nor to valorize a perceived social status of indigeneity, or to qualify essential differences between descendants of native Hawaiians and descendants of settlers. Rather, this paper is an effort to examine how contemporary legends told informally as true within folk groups negotiate native Hawaiian cultural values within the geocultural context of a multiethnic island population, many of whom have mixed ethnic ancestry, and who regardless of their own specific ethnicities convey ideas about the interconnectedness between land, people, and Hawaiian cultural values. This analytical approach will necessarily involve consideration of how storytellers express social anxieties about what it means to be "native" and what cultural authenticity is – a phenomenon not unique to Hawai'i. In many ways this study links to postcolonial experiences of place and identity in other island communities, in particular to the "islandic perspective" of perceiving island life as shaped in large part by the surrounding sea, and thus always-already as different from life on a continental landmass (Olwig, 2007: 262). As Adam Grydehøj (2013: 40) argues, "islanders themselves frequently conceive of their homes and cultures in opposition to or otherwise with reference to the outside world." In contemporary Hawai'i, the islandic perspective sees the 'mainland' (i.e. continental USA) as the geographically remote, but politically dominant place of difference that hegemonically posits island life and identity as inferior or "other" compared to mainstream USA. Hawai'i was an independent kingdom from 1810 to 1893, when a U.S.-backed coup d'etat led to annexation to the United States, despite "the existence of anti-annexation petitions and the large organizations that protested annexation" (Silva, 2004: 163). In 1959, Hawai'i became a U.S. state. Consequently, the U.S. mainland became Hawai'i's focal point of reference, although Hawai'i, being the geographical halfway point between Asia and North America, is also culturally attuned to and influenced by Asian cultures, particularly Japanese, Chinese, Korean, and Filipino, since the majority of Asian immigrants to Hawai'i have come from those countries. As Karen Fog Olwig (2007: 272) concludes in a study of Caribbean culture, "islands attain their meaning within a complex network of interrelationships that involves strong centrifugal as well as centripetal forces." Such complex interrelated cultural and social networks permeate everyday life in Hawai'i and contribute to the cultural complexity of folk beliefs and traditions of the supernatural. However, it appears that the emphasis on Hawaiian values and concepts in contemporary oral folk narratives reflects a cultural preference for centripetal cultural forces such as unity and a shared identity and experience of everyday life, including encounters with the supernatural, rather than with the centrifugal forces of cultural division that have led to ethnic tension and violence in Fiji, for example (Sriskandarajah, 2003; Narayan, 2008; Morgan, 2014). In significant ways, contemporary legends in Hawai'i sustain an idea of unified local identity, both in relation to Hawai'i vs. the mainland, but also in relation to local identities consisting of many multiethnic individuals as well as people embracing a single identity as native Hawaiians, descendants of settlers, or newcomers to the islands.

Moreover, a parallel to Olwig's observation on the cultural anxiety stemming from the tension between centripetal and centrifugal cultural forces can be seen in Hawai'i where the lingering effects of a cultural revival movement starting in the 1970s include the way people perceive of themselves as belonging, not only as citizens of Hawai'i in general, but connected to specific places in the islands. One of the reasons why stories of place are so important in Hawaiian culture is the belief that everyone has a *piko* (navel) in the landscape. Student Kawehiokaiulani Hanohano explains, "traditional Hawaiians conceived of their own personal identity as situated within their genealogy and *'aina hanau* [homeland]. Without one's *'ohana* [family] and *'aina* [land], one was without one's self." Starting in the 1970s, a renewed interest in Hawaiian language, traditions, and cultural practices like hula and long-distance canoe voyaging inspired the Hawaiian Renaissance movement and fueled political protests, including efforts to restore Hawaiian sovereignty and national independence, reclamation of land for public use, shoreline access for fishing and recreational purposes, rights to gather culturally significant plants on public and private lands, and, most importantly, the successful implementation of Hawaiian language immersion schools. From a cultural studies perspective, the Hawaiian Renaissance movement's centripetal forces embraced political stability, ethnic solidarity, and the spirit of *aloha*; however, the movement also created tensions, anxiety, and resentment amongst islanders who felt excluded from its focus on Hawaiian ethnicity. This propelled additional anxiety about already existing blood-quantum policies, which aimed – in the patronizing language of the United States Court of Appeals, Ninth Circuit – "to work for the betterment of Hawaiians" (Rice vs. Cayetano, 1998: n.p.). Said one man I interviewed, "I was born and raised in the islands. So were my parents, and so were their parents. But because I have no Hawaiian blood, I was unable to apply for scholarships for my own and my children's education and homestead lands for my family that only Hawaiians can apply for." In a different interview, a person of Hawaiian descent said, "there are historical and cultural reasons why Hawaiians should have certain privileges. We lost our land. We lost our kingdom. It's not fair that outsiders came and took it all away. We need help to move forward." The social tensions arising from the perceived ethnic discrimination and/or privileges based on genealogy contribute to the anxieties and dilemmas about racial identity expressed in chicken skin tales. To illustrate the cultural context briefly outlined here, I will summarize two of the most popular types of contemporary legends, which exist in many versions, both in print and orally. I will present versions of older and newer legends thematically rather than chronologically in order to highlight their thematic affinities. The first type of contemporary legend is about the ghost warriors colloquially known as "nightmarchers"; the second involves encounters with the volcano goddess Pele.

Nightmarchers: blood, mana, and masculinity
Nightmarchers refer to night processions of ghosts of Hawaiian warriors. The Hawaiian terms *huaka'i pō*, which means "night procession or parade" (Pukui & Elbert, 1986: 84), and *'oi'o*, which means "procession of ghosts of a departed chief and his company" (Pukui & Elbert ,1986: 280), evoke pre-colonial Hawai'i's political structure of ruling chiefs and their powerful privileges. More symbolically, nightmarcher legends establish respect for culture-based authority and imbue Hawaiian masculinity, which is reduced to a subservient position in the tourism-driven economy of contemporary Hawai'i, with power and awe. In Hawaiian culture, night (*pō*) is associated with "darkness, obscurity; the realm of the gods, chaos, or hell" (Pukui & Elbert, 1986: 333), with prophetic visions and dreams, and with spirits, death, and sickness. "Those who took part in the march were the chiefs and warriors who had died, the *aumakua* [personal guardian spirits], and the gods, each of whom had their own march" (Beckwith, 2007: 198).

Social and political life in pre-colonial Hawai'i was structured by an elaborate system of rules (*kapu* = taboos, prohibitions) that governed everyday relations between men and women, *kānaka* or *maka'āinana* (commoners) and *alii* (chiefs). Violating taboos was a serious matter, especially when commoners infringed on chiefs' privileges. "The punishment inflicted on those who violated the tabu of the chiefs was to be burned with fire until their bodies were reduced to ashes, or to be strangled, or stoned to death. Thus it was that the tabus of the chiefs oppressed the whole people" (Malo, 1951: 57). The chiefs obtained their rank-specific taboos as a result of their bloodline or through extraordinary feats in battle. A low-ranking war chief might through military prowess successfully graft himself onto a high-ranking bloodline via marriage, but he could never obtain the true *mana*, that is, the authority of sacred power and pure blood that the sacred chiefs possessed exclusively through their genealogy.

While echoes of the privileges associated with bloodline can be detected in contemporary nightmarcher narratives, so can the awe and fear evoked by the legendary Hawaiian warrior, a popular symbol of hypermasculinity, power, and the perceived glory of ancient Hawai'i. In the oral stories collected by students, nightmarchers are described as very tall (always 6 ft. or taller) and muscular – and always male. However, in older printed versions, there are both male and female nightmarchers (Beckwith, 2007). This correlates with the contemporary nation-centered validation of Hawaiian masculinity through traditional tattoos, the revitalization of Hawaiian martial arts, canoe paddling, and *koa* (warriorhood, bravery) that "have become key sites for the re-membering of Hawaiian cultural masculinities as decolonizing practice" (Tengan, 2008: 43). The narratives' emphasis on the authority-wielding nightmarchers' aggressive masculinity thus constructs an indigenous male identity vastly different from the smiling, servile, ukulele-playing, effeminate male islander that tourists encounter in Hawai'i's hospitality industry.

Nightmarchers are sometimes heralded by chanting, drumming, or the blowing of the conch shell (*pu*), an eerie sound that carries far and was used ceremonially in pre-colonial Hawai'i to announce the approach of chiefs. Some people report seeing lit torches carried by the nightmarchers. "I hear them all the time," a woman who had moved to Pahoa from the mainland complained, "All that drumming and chanting. It drives me crazy." In the contemporary stories collected by students, the drumming and chanting are represented as uncanny and unnerving. Older print sources suggest a more symbiotic acceptance of these vestiges of ancient Hawaiian culture: "Mrs. Emma Akana Olmsted tells me […] now that she is older and can herself actually hear [the nightmarchers] she is no longer afraid. She hears beautiful loud chanting of voices, the high notes of the flute and drumming so loud that it seems beaten upon the side of the house beside her bed" (Beckwith, 2007: 200).

However, both contemporary oral narratives and older print sources emphasize the importance of blood relations between the ghost warriors and people in the present. This eyewitness account, collected by Martha Beckwith (2007: 100) in the 1930s, appears in *Kepelino's Traditions of Hawaii*:

A young man of Kona, Hawai'i, tells the following experience:

One night just after nightfall, about seven or eight in the evening, he was on his way when of a sudden he saw a long line of marchers in the distance coming toward him. He climbed over a stone wall and sat very still. As they drew near he saw that they walked four abreast and were about seven feet tall nor did their feet touch the ground. One of the marchers stepped out of the line and ran back and forth on the other side of the wall behind where he crouched as if to protect him from the others. As each file passed he heard voices call out "Strike!' and his protector answered, "No! no! he is mine!" No other sounds were to be heard except the call to strike and the creak of a *ma-ne-le* [sedan chair]. He was not afraid and watched the marchers closely. There were both men and women in the procession. After a long line of marchers four abreast had passed there came the *ma-ne-le* bearers, two before and two behind. On the litter sat a very big man whom he guessed at once to be a chief. Following the litter were other marchers walking four abreast. After all had passed, his protector joined his fellows.

In comparison, none of my students collected nightmarcher stories that featured a chief on a litter or women warriors, but the emphasis on eeriness and bloodline prevailed. A student related that his Hawaiian grandfather had decided to tear down the back section of his house near Kawaihae because of what he called "da night walkers." Their path went through that part of the house, and he saw no other option than to tear it down and rebuild it on the other side of the house. The back of his house faced a steep gulch, which according to legend had been the home of chiefs and warriors in the old days. The young man asked his grandfather if the nightmarchers might harm them. "No," said the old man, speaking in HCE, "dey no harm you 'cause you 'ohana [family]. Dat means you're in da line" (i.e. belong to their bloodline).

It is considered notoriously dangerous to encounter the nightmarchers. Some students report that you may go insane. Others have heard of people who died of fright. Rick Carroll has recorded an anonymous eyewitness account in which a foolhardy German who, while visiting relatives on the island of O'ahu, decided to follow the sound of drums coming from a mountain cave in the back of a valley. (Hawaiians often used caves for burials and for that reason they are still considered *kapu*). The German did not return. "At daylight they went looking for him. They found him in the middle of the trail with his mouth wide open and his eyes wide open, and his fingers bent back, and apparently dead of a heart attack" (Carroll, 1972: 107-108). The clash between Hawaiian and western interpretations of cause of death finds expression here. Mary Kawena Wiggin Pukui explains, "If a man is found stricken by the roadside a white doctor will pronounce the cause as heart failure, but a

Hawaiian will think at once of the fatal night marchers" (Beckwith, 2007: 198). But as stated in the stories from Kona and Kawaihae, being related to one of the ghost warriors can save you. Lopaka Kapanui explains, "your best chance is to have an ancestor who recognizes you and calls out, 'Na'u!' which means 'Mine!' [e.g. belonging to me]. If you are in the nightmarcher's bloodline, no one in the procession can harm you" (2005:58).

Again, the privileges and *mana* associated with genealogy prevail. In case you cannot establish such a tie, the next best thing, according to the oral narratives my students collected, is to show respect. This needs to follow ritual protocol reminiscent of the *kapu*, or taboo, system in pre-contact Hawaii. Social rank outlined all interpersonal relationships. The ruling chiefs were believed to possess various degrees of *mana*, i.e. supernatural or divine power, which gave them authority and entitled them to privileges. People of inferior rank were not allowed to touch, look at, or in any way interfere with the ruling chiefs or what belonged to them. It was even taboo for a commoner's shadow to fall on a chief (Malo, 1951: 56). To break the *kapu* meant instant "death by burning"; however, when a taboo breaker was about to be killed, chiefs of the same rank as the one whose taboo had been broken could release the offender so that "he would not die, but would live" (Kamakau, 1964: 10). The option for clemency also exists in contemporary nightmarcher lore, but only if the offender is a blood relation of one of the marchers. In nightmarcher lore collected in Ka'u in the 1930s by Mary Kawena Wiggin Pukui, the *aumakua* (guardian spirits) in the nightmarcher procession were believed to "protect their living progeny" (Beckwith, 2007: 198); in contrast, today's nightmarcher lore emphasizes the protection of bloodline rather than guardian spirits.

Students reported that there are three basic ways to show respect and hence avoid the nightmarchers' wrath. One is to not look: if you encounter the nightmarchers, it is best to turn your back to them and run away as quickly as possible. The second option is to prostrate yourself before them, face down, not looking at them. Several students stated that it was advisable to remove all your clothing as a sign of humility before prostrating yourself. Of course, the advice to strip down is given with a bit of nervous laughter, but the essence of not challenging authority with direct eye contact and of showing respect and humility by prostrating on the ground in a position of naked surrender suggests the haunting presence of the Hawaiian *kapu* system. In pre-colonial Hawai'i, the *kapu moe* (prostration taboo) only belonged to the three highest ranks of chiefs, the *niaupio*, the *pio*, and the *naha*, whose bloodlines were considered the purest and most sacred (Malo, 1951: 57; Kamakau, 1964: 4-5). Additionally, the practice of kowtowing as a sign of reverence was familiar to the Chinese immigrants in Hawai'i, many of whom intermarried with native Hawaiians. So, while it is tempting to interpret chicken skin tales exclusively in relation to pre-contact Hawaiian cultural practices, these stories often have multicultural dimensions. Still, the insistence in the nightmarcher stories on blood ties to the past is quite remarkable and underscores the perceived inequality expressed by many contemporary Hawai'i residents regarding legislation and institutional practices that favor residents with a certain native Hawaiian blood quantum.

According to several female students, the third option of avoiding being harmed by nightmarchers has to do with the person's sex: the only people safe from the nightmarchers' harm are menstruating women. A young Hawaiian woman who was camping with friends in Waipio Valley, a place notoriously haunted by nightmarchers, told me, "it's true! The Hawaiians were very strict about girls on their periods. The blood was seen as a sickness, and if it dropped somewhere important (like in the *loi/mala* [soil], where *kalo* [taro] is grown) that place would be contaminated. In the case of the nightmarchers, a *ma'i wahine* [menstruating woman] was considered too dirty to touch, and I would have been passed over, as I had been on my period." David Malo (1951: 29) writes that it was taboo for men to have sexual relations with menstruating women. "A flowing woman was looked upon as both unclean and unlucky." Furthermore, because women were considered ritually unclean, men and women ate separately, only men prepared the food, and "certain foods were denied to women by reason of their sex" (Handy & Pukui, 1998: 177). From a western perspective, these practices may appear as a cultural devaluation of women and gender-politically as sexist prejudice against women, but the local women I spoke with (both Hawaiian and of mixed ethnicity) were unconcerned about such negative interpretations. Instead, several of them expressed pride in the reproductive power of women and regarded menstruation as a symbol of that. One joked, "It just goes to show how weak and vulnerable men are that they cannot touch us when our blood is flowing." In the following discussion of Pele lore, it will become apparent that women are in fact seen as very powerful in Hawaiian culture and that there exists a great deal of ambiguity about the supposed inferiority of women's social status.

However, it is one thing to encounter nightmarchers accidentally, and quite another to cohabit with them. Several students had collected stories about ghost warriors marching through houses. In the Kawaihae story cited above, the owner opted to tear down part of the house. In the following story, which took place near Onomea Bay outside Hilo, a local Japanese student's elderly aunt and uncle's house was haunted by nightmarchers. Large, fearsome-looking men with black or tattooed faces, carrying clubs, would march single-file through the house on certain nights. They would walk right through the walls, never knocking down anything, but leaving the old people sleepless and frustrated. The couple asked for spiritual help from a Shinto priest. But no matter the number of prayers and blessings, the nightmarchers kept marching. Finally, on the advice of a kindly Hawaiian neighbor, they asked a Hawaiian *kahuna* - "priest, sorcerer, magician, wizard, minister" (Pukui & Elbert, 1986: 114) - for help. He surveyed the land around the house and determined that it was built right on the nightmarchers' trail. He performed several rites of making the house taboo for the nightmarchers by chanting, sprinkling Hawaiian salt, and planting *ti* plants (*cordyline fruticosa*), all of which are believed to ward off evil spirits. Many houses in Hawai'i, including my own, have a row of *ti* plants in the garden. The ritual and medicinal uses of salt to cleanse places and bodies of illness and bad energy hark back to pre-contact Hawai'i, and so does the importance placed on interacting with the supernatural in specific locations. Contemporary nightmarcher lore thus *ho'omau* (perpetuates) and validates cultural practices that reinforce a local identity in relation to place and tradition. As Michel de Certeau observes, tales "frequently reverse the relationships of power" (1984: 23), allowing cultural values largely ignored in dominant culture to percolate and find expression in folk beliefs.

Pele: Land, pork, and female empowerment
While nightmarcher lore is concerned with the privileges of genealogy, *mana* (sacred power), and masculinity, contemporary legends involving the volcano goddess Pele express contemporary folk beliefs about the sacredness of the land and fear of the unpredictable volcano goddess. Although oral narratives about encounters with nightmarchers and Pele exist on all the Hawaiian Islands, Pele is specifically associated with the Puna and Ka'u districts on the island of Hawai'i, which are home to the active

Kīlauea and Mauna Loa volcanoes. Pele is known in Hawaiian mythology as the destroyer and creator of land. Temperamental, jealous and easily angered, Pele commands the land and is personified through the earthquakes and volcanic eruptions that continuously transform the landscape. In Hawaiian, the name Pele means "lava flow, volcano, eruption" (Pukui & Elbert, 1986: 323). While Pele is considered a lesser deity in the Hawaiian pantheon and organized Pele worship no longer exists, people still offer alcohol, tobacco, food, and other consumable items to her in times of volcanic eruptions. Significantly, she is the most regularly sighted Hawaiian deity. H. Arlo Nimmo (1986: 123) summarizes:

> Sometimes she is a beautiful young woman dressed in flowing red or white, while at other times she is an ugly old crone, decrepit and ragged – both traditional guises of Pele. But whatever the guise, she is the volcano goddess en route to the volcanoes to stir up activity. Sometimes she is simply seen by someone, sometimes she asks for food or lodging, at other times she is hitchhiking and offered a ride, during which she may engage in conversation, and almost always, she mysteriously disappears after or during the encounters.

Although women in pre-contact Hawai'i in general were considered *noa* – "common, profane, or perhaps more accurately 'free of kapu'" (Linnekin, 1990: 13) – it is noteworthy that contemporary legends about the volcano goddess Pele are concerned with different kinds of taboo breaking than nightmarcher legends are. The taboos mentioned in contemporary Pele legends are a mixture of ancient and hybrid cultural values. They particularly concern the *kapu* about taking pork across the mountains and the norms pertaining to hospitality and generosity. Furthermore, in contrast to nightmarcher lore, which tends to focus on the power, hypermasculinity, and *mana* of the Hawaiian chiefs, and which might function as cautionary reminders of the violent customs of the past, many versions of contemporary legends involving the volcano goddess Pele show a larger degree of cultural hybridity. For example, there is considerable overlap in Pele lore with popular American contemporary legends such as the vanishing hitchhiker (Brunvand, 1981). However, contemporary Pele lore disrupts western perceptions of the female gender as lesser or "other" by positing the female principle as parallel, perhaps even superior, to the political world controlled by men. Pele's spectacular eruptive energy is both destructive and constructive, but never under the reign of male authority. The following example of a Pele hitchhiker legend collected by a female student demonstrates these characteristics:

My uncle was going nightfishing in Ka'u. As he was driving past the volcano [Kīlauea], he saw someone standing on the side of the road. It was really dark, and he didn't want to pick up some crazy hippie. But when he came closer, he saw that it was a woman, real good-looking, in a tight white dress. She had long black hair and sleek brown skin. She was real good looking. He thought to himself, "shoots!" He was happy. He pulled right over and picked her up. She only wanted to sit on the backseat. They drove along. He felt real good about having such a good-looking chick in the car with him. She said she was going to Pahala. Then she asked him for a cigarette. He said, "sorry, but I no smoke." Then she became real quiet. My uncle felt kind of uneasy. When he glanced at her in the rearview mirror, she suddenly looked much older. Her eyes looked weird, sort of smoldering, or glowing faintly. He got so freaked out he nearly crashed the car. He managed to pull over and stop on the side of the road. When he turned around to look at her, she was gone. He was sure it had been Pele.

The motifs of Pele's sudden appearance and disappearance, and her ability to shape shift from sexy young woman to ugly old crone

[131]

are common plot elements. Unlike the nightmarchers, who are described as fierce and unapproachable, Pele is usually described as interacting with people and testing their generosity. The majority of the stories features Pele as a hitchhiker on desolate stretches of road around the volcano, and like American hitchhiker legends there is a subtext of fear of strangers and death, though not for random but for cultural reasons, such as breaking the taboo against taking pork across the mountains. A student collected this story from his aunt, which has many versions in Pele literature:

I was driving across the Saddle Road when suddenly my car wen' stall. It had just been serviced and was in good condition. But it died just lik' dat! And there I was! No more cell phone reception, no cars, no mo' nothing. Just the fog and the lava fields. Then I remembered: I had pork in the car, 'cause I was going to my mother's house, see, with food for my nephew's baby *luau* [party], and we was going fo' make *kalua* pork and cabbage. Ho! Once I wen' realize what I did wrong, I got out of the car, opened the cooler with all the food, and I threw out all the pork, while I said, "sorry, tutu [grandmother], sorry, I never meant no harm". And right away my car wen' start again.

Pork was among the foods that women were not allowed to eat in pre-contact Hawai'i. The eating taboos (*'ai kapu*), which prohibited men and women from eating together and women from preparing food, have long been abandoned, but the power of the pork taboo still haunts the geocultural imaginary in Hawai'i. Numerous stories warn people about taking pork across the mountains. They echo the ancient eating taboos and are seen as showing lack of respect for Pele, the female divine, who rules over the mountain areas. The car may stall or crash, unusual winds may suddenly occur, and bad luck will haunt offenders. A student concludes, "I believe these warnings are important because they teach us how to behave:

appropriately, honorably and respectfully, to be upstanding citizens. Also, these warnings teach us how important it is to know your friends from your enemies."

Pele is also known to enter homes and ask for lodging, food, or drink (including alcohol). A student reported that once when she was a child, she saw an old lady sit in a chair in her uncle's house in Kalapana late at night. The old lady asked for a drink. The girl gave her water, but the old lady told her to get gin instead. There was no gin in the house; however, the old lady was satisfied when she was offered whiskey. The next day, the volcano erupted, but the uncle's house was not touched by the lava flow. Another student stated that his aunt in Waimea had been approached by a strange little girl, while she was preparing a meal in the kitchen. The girl asked for a glass of water. She drank the whole glass down in one gulp, and when she handed it back to the woman, the glass was icy on the outside. Soon there was an earthquake, but the woman's house was not damaged. Such narratives reinforce the belief that Pele will protect your property if you treat her well. Hospitality, politeness, and above all respect for the land are some of the values in Pele stories. One man declared, "Pele is the mother for us Hawaiians. She deserves respect."

Having bad luck is associated with not having shown proper respect. A woman from Opihikao said, "I have heard too many stories of people being plagued by bad luck: car trouble and accidents, fatal illness and disabilities, unexplainable negative occurrences and general unhappiness. All happening after something associated with Pele was taken." For example, it is considered bad luck to pick up lava rocks as souvenirs, or to remove stones that have a special connection to a place. Children learn to respect the land and to care for it early on. Several of my students reported having been disciplined by their elders for playing with lava rocks, especially in the volcano area. In other instances, they are taught to care for the land and to *malama* the *aina* by planting coconuts, *ti* plants, and other edible plants on land overrun by lava. A student explains, "If we *malama* the *'aina* (take care of the land), it's going to feed us, it's going to nurture us, and it's going to give us life."

Understanding and accepting the constantly forming and transforming volcanic landscape also find expression in contemporary Pele lore. If the volcano erupts, there is no point in resisting it. Emma Kapunohu'ulaokalani Kauhi, who grew up under the volcano in Kalapana, relates, "My mother had told me, 'When Pele comes, let her have the land. She made this land. She'll be here forever. You and I will be here only temporarily.' When I asked her, 'What about the house?' She answered, 'Let her have it'" (Kauhi, 2000: 134-135). As oral narratives such as these suggest, the apparent devaluation of women in Hawaiian culture should be considered in juxtaposition to the cultural valuation of the female divine, who creates, destroys, and recreates the land. Where nightmarchers appear as a collective masculine unit to protect blood-related kin and reinforce the power of the chiefs, Pele singularly controls the land. Sometimes benign, sometimes wrathful, Pele remains the ultimate manifestation of the female divine in contemporary chicken skin stories.

Concluding perspectives on contemporary nightmarcher and Pele lore
Contemporary chicken skin stories from the island of Hawai'i pose multiple perspectives on islanders' shared cultural values and anxieties. While embracing Hawaiian cultural values has the centripetal effects of reinforcing cultural admiration, respect, and nostalgia for pre-colonial Hawai'i, the anxiety about colonial identity and racial and ethnic discrimination in contemporary Hawai'i lurks within these unmediated expressions of folklore.

The native Hawaiian population has been in steady decline since the earliest contact with Europeans. In a provocative and influential book, *And Then There Were None*, Martha Noyes (2003: 11) tracks the decline in the number of "pure Hawaiians" during the last two hundred years. In a foreword to Noyes' book, Elizabeth Kapu'uwailani Lindsey Buyers expresses the experience of alienation and disconnection from the land that many Hawaiians feel. She applauds Noyes' "effort to give voice to *kupuna* [ancestors] who became strangers in their own land, a land that once nourished their dreams and now cradle their bones. Without these stories, Hawai'i's history is incomplete" (2003: vi). The sense of loss stemming from the decline in the number of pure-blooded native Hawaiians is further acerbated by the fact that native blood quantum is used institutionally and legally by the Federal Government, the court system, the State of Hawai'i, Office of Hawaiian Affairs, and the prestigious Kamehameha Schools. Thus, Hawaiian blood becomes a source of both power and mystery because it establishes a person's entitlements in the present via bloodlines to the past. However, not all agree. J. Kehaulani Kauanui (2008: 15) argues:

Hawaiians' traditional form of considering who belongs and who descends from the *'aina* (land) relies on bilateral descent over and above constructions of blood quantum. [...] Yet many point to Hawaiian racial mixedness - a result of this incorporation, often through intermarriage - as evidence of indigenous dissolution instead of a sign of cultural resilience. Only by ignoring Hawaiian genealogical practices could exogamy be viewed as a one-way road to cultural disappearance, where racial purity is confused with survival and leads to an assumption of inevitable decline.

The contrast between Noyes' perception of loss of ethnic purity, which results in cultural decline, and Kauanui's assertion that Hawaiian identity and culture are perpetuated in Hawai'i's multiethnic population, is at the heart of the cultural anxiety permeating contemporary ghost lore in Hawaii. This tug between centrifugal and centripetal forces of cultural cohesion and islanders' shared identity finds dynamic expression in contemporary folk beliefs and oral narratives, where nightmarcher lore sustains perceptions of bloodline, power, and submission to authority, while Pele lore emphasizes the importance of acceptance, generosity, caring, and showing *aloha*. The haunting of the past, both Hawaii's colonial history with its racial inequalities and cultural transformations, and the phantoms of its more distant pre-colonial past with its rich mythology and dramatic legends, inform nightmarcher and Pele lore and sustain a geocultural imaginary subversive to the metahistories imposed on Hawai'i from outside. As contemporary legends, chicken skin stories create social spaces within which cultural values, traditions, and histories find meaningful expression.

References

Beckwith, M.W. (Ed.). 2007. *Kepelino's Traditions of Hawaii.* Honolulu: Bishop Museum Bulletin, 95.

Bennett, G. & Smith, P. (Eds.). 1996. *Contemporary Legend: A Reader.* New York: Garland.

Brunvand, J.H. 1981. *The Vanishing Hitchhiker: American Urban Legends and Their Meanings.* New York: W. W. Norton.

Brunvand, J.H. 1999. *Too Good to Be True: The Colossal Book of Urban Legends.* New York: W. W. Norton & Co.

Campion-Vincent, V. 2005. From Evil Others to Evil Elites: A Dominant Pattern in Conspiracy Theories Today. In: G.A. Fine (Ed.), *Rumor Mills: The Social Impact of Rumor and Legend.* New Brunswick, NJ: Transaction, pp. 103-122.

Carroll, R. 1997. *Chicken Skin. True Spooky Stories of Hawai'i.* Honolulu: Bess Press.

Certeau, M.d. 1984. *The Practice of Everyday Life.* Berkeley: University of California Press.

DeBlasio, D.M et al. 2009. *CatchingStories: A Practical Guide to Oral History*. Athens: Ohio University Press.

Dégh, L. 2001. *Legend and Belief: Dialectics of a Folklore Genre*. Bloomington: Indiana University Press.

Glassie, H. 1995. Tradition. In: *The Journal of American Folklore*, 108 (430), pp. 395-412.

Goldstein, D. 2004. *Once Upon a Virus: AIDS Legends and Vernacular Risk Perception*. Logan: Utah State University Press.

Grydehøj, A. 2013. Ethnicity and the Origins of Local Identity in Shetland, UK – Part I: Picts, Vikings, Fairies, Finns, and Aryans. In: *Journal of Marine and Island Cultures*, 2, pp. 39-48.

Handy, E.S.C. & Pukui, M.K. 1998. *The Polynesian Family System in Ka'u, Hawai'i*. Honolulu: Mutual Publishing.

Kamakau, S. M. [1866-1871] 1964. *Ka Po'e Kahiko: The People of Old*. M.K. Pukui (Transl.). Honolulu: Bishop Museum Press.

Kapanui, L. 2005. *Haunted Hawaiian Nights*. Honolulu: Mutual.

Kauhi, E.K. 2000. *He Mo'olelo No Kapa'ahu*. C. M. Langlas (Transl.). Hilo: Pili Productions.

Kauanui, J. K. 2008. *Hawaiian Blood: Colonialism and the Politics of Sovereignty and Indigeneity*. Durham: Duke University Press.

Klintberg, B.a. 1986. *Råttan i pizzan: Folksägner i vår tid*. Stockholm: Norstedts.

Linnekin, J. 1990. *Sacred Queens and Women of Consequence: Rank, Gender, and Colonialism in the Hawaiian Islands*. Ann Arbor: University of Michigan Press.

Malo, David. [1898] 1951. *Hawaiian Antiquities [Moolelo Hawaii]*. N. B. Emerson (Transl.). Honolulu: Bishop Museum Press.

Morgan, R. 2014. Living Water: Christian Theologies and Interethnic Relations in Fiji. In: *Asia Pacific Journal of Anthropology* 15 (1), pp. 65-84.

Narayan, S. 2008. Racial Discrimination in Fiji. In: *Journal of South Pacific Law* 12 (1), pp. 68-75.

Nimmo, H.A. 1986. Pele, Ancient Goddess of Contemporary Hawaii. In: *Pacific Studies* 9 (2), pp. 121-179.

Noyes, M. 2003. *And Then There Were None*. Honolulu: Bess Press.

Olwig, K.F. 2007. Islands as Places of Being and Belonging. In: *Geographical Review* 97 (2), pp. 260-273.

Pukui, M. K. & Elbert, S. H. 1986. *Hawaiian Dictionary*. Honolulu: University of Hawaii Press.

Rice vs. Cayetano. 1998. United States Court of Appeals. Ninth Circuit. No. 97-16095.

Silva, N.K. 2004. *Aloha Betrayed: Native Hawaiian Resistance to American Colonialism*. Durham: Duke University Press.

Sriskandarajah, D. 2003. Inequality and Conflict in Fiji: From Purgatory to Hell? In: *Asia Pacific Viewpoint* 44 (3), pp. 305-324.

Tengan, T. P. K. 2008. Re-Membering Panala'au: Masculinities, Nation, and Empire in Hawai'i and the Pacific. In: *The Contemporary Pacific* 20 (1), pp. 27-53.

Tonouchi, L. 2005. *Da Kine Dictionary. Compiled and Edited by Lee A. Tonouchi*. Honolulu: Bess Press.

Chapter 6
Reports of the Supernatural in Genealogy

Barbara Annan
Independent Folklore Researcher, USA (PhD, Depth Psychology)

Introduction
Uncanny experiences that occur during genealogical research have not been an area of much attention in Folklore Studies. In fact a sizable sub-culture of genealogists speak guardedly of experiences of coincidence, hunches, intuition, and feelings of being 'guided' by the spirits of the deceased.

This is a report primarily focusing on a personal interview with a percipient who is a respected professional genealogist and a Fellow in the American Association of Genealogists, Henry Z. Jones, Jr. Jones has published two volumes of oral narratives related to him by genealogists; *Psychic Roots: Serendipity & Intuition in Genealogy* (1993) and *Psychic Roots: Further Adventures in Serendipity and Intuition in Genealogy* (1997). These volumes provide a secondary source for this study. The following describes and places into a folkloric framework several types of supernatural or uncanny experiences that ancestry researchers describe and examines how the percipients understand their paranormal experiences.

Virtanen (1977) writes of psychic experiences: "Informatory experiences are a remarkable feature of our culture. [...] The standard world view prevalent in our society offers no places for such experiences." A search for meaning and affirmation for such experiences has created a sub-culture and "specialized vocabulary"

(Bennett, 1995) among a minority of genealogists. Further, drawing on the 'legend tripping' concept of Bill Ellis (2004) and the theories of liminality and rites of passage described by Victor Turner (1987) and Arnold van Gennep (1908), I propose the possibility of a quasi-shamanic role simulated in the paranormal experiences of genealogical research, when feeling they are being 'helped' by the dead ancestors, as are shamans. The percipients report incidents of déjà vu, predictive dreams, and uncanny coincidences as they focus their work in threshold areas between the living and the deceased.

Curiosity about this topic stirred for this writer while reading about the adolescent rite of passage that folklorist Bill Ellis (2004: 114) describes as 'legend tripping' or ostention. This well-documented practice includes cemetery visits made by adolescents as a rite of passage, involving a daring night excursion to try to relive a haunting or evoke a spirit. Another, older cohort also linger for hours in graveyards. These are the tombstone-seeking ancestry researchers.

Currently, amateur genealogists, often retired 'baby boomers', who have the time and money, are seeking their progenitors. They are wending their ways across America or boarding planes to ancestral lands to seek family names in cemeteries and musty archives. They are prepared to spend long, lonely hours seeking specific gravestones, meditating on the long dead.

A memorate (a term coined by the Swedish folklorist Carl Wilhelm von Sydow) illustrating the supernatural lore coincident with seeking the ancestors was related to me by a middle-aged couple, who after retirement became genealogy hobbyists. Wayne and Andrea made a trip from Alaska to North Dakota to find the grave of Wayne's forbearers. They arrived at a deserted cemetery with no map of the graves, tired from the drive. They were dismayed by the enormity of the task to find one grave marker among hundreds. While Wayne stood by the motorhome, Andrea went to stretch her legs. She strode randomly among the graves, suddenly stopping with a gasp. "I can't believe it!" she called out, " Your Uncle Bill's right here by my feet!" What were the odds of her finding her husband's ancestor so quickly, they wondered? They were awestruck and in their words, "Weirded out" by the event. I wondered how common this type of occurrence was.

A cursory Internet search revealed that versions of this story have almost become 'urban legend' among ancestry researchers. It is a familiar theme, widely retold and claimed by many narrators as a personal, original story. The Internet also provides a growing number of websites containing stories of genealogical supernatural or anomalous experiences. Genealogy Forum News, Genealogy-wise, www.squidoo.com, and several individual ancestry web pages and blogs include personal narratives on paranormal experiences.

My initial research efforts to reach out to genealogists had mixed results. A query about coincidence, intuition, or odd experiences was met with skepticism, humour, incredulity at the suggestion, and occasionally a shared story that began, "I don't know what to make of this, but..." or "This is not something I usually share..."

I had expected some disinterest, but I also found negative reactions. My first direct query letter to a professional genealogist returned a sharp response. This well-established researcher stated she was "taken aback" by my e-mail. She said, "I see genealogy as a logic puzzle. I do not think the dead spirits play any role" (personal correspondence, 2012).

A book by Anne Bradshaw, *True Miracles with Genealogy: Help from the Beyond* (2010), affirmed that there are genealogists willing to testify publicly to their belief in supernatural help. This book by a member of the Church of Latter-Day Saints is a collection of stories of feelings of being helped or guided by unseen presences. Bradshaw's work is self-published and has a personal bias, what Folklorist David Hufford (2010: 144) calls, "interpretive spiritual experience," not because it has the features of the supernatural experience itself, but because it is viewed in the light of a prior religious framework. Bradshaw interprets the events as intentionally bringing the ancestors into reconciliation with the living as predicted by Elijah the Prophet. Bradshaw's work is worth noting, but I chose to work with better documented and less religiously laden memorates. The primary resources chosen for this paper were an interview with Henry Z. Jones, Jr., and his works on para-normal experiences among professional genealogists; *Psychic Roots: Serendipity & Intuition in Genealogy* (1993) and *Psychic Roots: Further Adventures in Serendipity and Intuition in Genealogy* (1997). These books are without overtones from any one religion. They are presented as two volumes of collections of well-documented narratives. It is published by a respected organization, the Genealogical Publishing Company.

Jones is a Fellow of the American Association of Genealogists and a respected author of several volumes on the immigration of the Palatine Germans. Of primary interest to this study was his informal survey of 300 certified genealogists. Over 200 replied to his queries. All were English-speaking, professional genealogists: Australians, Canadians, and British as well as Americans. Almost all of the 200 respondents reported some sort of supernatural occurrence. This percentage approximates the findings of the 2005 Gallup poll, which reported that 3 out of 4 of Americans believe in some form of the supernatural. The stories of uncanny experiences while doing genealogy research and Jones' personal commentary and observations, are the material I draw from.

In April 2012, I interviewed Henry Jones, 'Hank', as he asked me to call him. We met in his favourite San Diego diner, the Hob Nob Cafe. He was open and forthcoming about his background and beliefs. Many of the anecdotes he told me were also in his books and had been reiterated in his frequent talks and seminars. It was not until we covered less rehearsed and more current material that I began to glimpse the gravity and depth of emotion Jones carries for his exploration of paragenealogy. Jones's professional attention to detail and his nonjudgmental attitude of "I don't know… I am a conduit, a collector of material," made him, in my opinion, an ideal resource for this study. The quotations with page citations are from his first paragenealogy book, *Psychic Roots: Serendipity and Intuition in Genealogy*. Quotes without citations are from the interview.

Jones grew up in San Leandro, California, and currently lives outside of San Diego. After majoring in communications with a minor in history at Stanford, Jones had a successful career in Hollywood music and films as a character actor. He married twice and has a daughter from the first marriage. Regarding his underlying beliefs, Jones is the only child of "strong Methodist" parents, which he states with a smile, has led him to seek therapy.

"I am not very much of a religious person," he said. His mother believed that there are, "many paths to God." "A lot of my therapy was getting away from the Methodist background. If I hadn't had therapy, I wouldn't have felt the freedom to be here and talk about these things." His beliefs, as he enters his seventh decade of life, have become inclusive and positive. He comments simply, "My spiritual view is that there is a God."

But what was it that led him to believe in supernatural phenomena that guide genealogists? During the interview, Jones related the following memorate of his first supernatural experience during his research on 847 Palatine families. He instructed his German researcher, Carla Mittelstaedt-Kubaseck, to begin her initial investigations by looking for one specific family out of the 847: the 1709er family of Dietrich Schneider:

I can't really say why I found this Schneider so interesting, but he always seemed to hold a strange fascination for me whenever I ran across his name in the old source materials. Little did I know that this impromptu decision ... was to be my introduction to what some have called 'The Twilight Zone of Genealogy' when unexplainable events and serendipitous experiences sometimes open doors and help us successfully find our ancestors. Even now I get chills down my spine as I try to fathom what occurred (Jones 1993: 14).

The search eventually located 600 of the 847 families. "And the only one I find that I am directly related to is the Dietrich Schneider family of Westerwald - my first choice selected *totally at random*" (1993: 14-15). This was when Jones became convinced that something out-of-the-ordinary was occurring. Jones added that at times during the work he dreamed of Palatines coming to redirect him when he was looking for information in the wrong place. When he re-directed his search he found what he was looking for immediately, giving him pause. He began to wonder about these experiences.

I asked if he had psychic experiences outside of his genealogical research. He responded with an account of his childhood nightly "flying" out-of-body experiences early in life and growing up with a grandmother who was respected for her psychic gifts.

The field of genealogy has been a life-long passion for Jones, beginning with documenting the Palatines, a group of immigrants from the Paltz region (hence 'Palatine') of Germany, who came to colonial America. *The Palatine Families of New York: A Study of the German Immigrants Who Arrived in New York in 1710* (1985). This work won the Donald Lines Jacobus Award for sound scholarship in genealogical writing. His careful efforts have resulted in several other books, including the *Palatine Families of Ireland* (1990) on Germans who stopped short of New York and stayed in Ireland, *Westerwald to America* (2000), and *More Palatine Families* (1991). During the years of research, Jones began to trust the feeling of being guided, led, or "nudged" to look further or in unlikely places for information. In time, he began to mention these odd coincidences in his seminars. The responses he received affirmed that he was not alone in his paranormal experiences.

Credibility was always one of Jones's foremost concerns. He made every effort to keep his exploration of psychic phenomena within the rigid demands of the scientific field of documentation that genealogy represents. He conducted his survey of psychic incidents methodically by sending out letters to 300 noted genealogists around the world. Over 200 replied, and he claimed that there were "no negative responses." I pursued this by saying, "I'm not sure what you mean by negative." He responded, "Well, I mean, like really saying, 'Get off it! Don't write the book. You're crazy'... that kind of thing. Nothing. Nothing like that kind of thing. Some said, 'I really don't have anything to contribute, cause I can't; I'm not into it. If it did happen, I don't remember it'" (Interview, 2012). As Jones wrote in 1993:

> Only one less-than enthusiastic response was received. It came from an editor of a prestigious journal who had published some of my Palatine material and book reviews. She was concerned that my new book might send mixed signals to less-experienced family historians and feared that the tabloids might sensationalize and distort my project with headlines such as 'Astrology Genealogy Recommended by Internationally-Known Genealogist' (Jones, 1993: 21).

Jones (1993: 21) comments that prior to the mailing he prepared himself for "the possibility of ridicule" from some of his colleagues.

His standing with the American Association of Professional Genealogists was at stake as well. The professional credibility of reputable genealogists lies in precise, logical work. It is reasonable for them to avoid topics that might call their profession into question. Jones cautioned that there is a "red flag" to avoid. He warned:

> There is a stigma to the word 'psychic'. There is such a flakiness to it. Anybody would think this is really weird, plus the whole area of mediums and all the way back to Houdini, exposing a lot of them, there's an awful lot of charlatans in that whole area who take advantage of people who are vulnerable. It's just not a nice thing to do, but they do it (Interview, 2012).

Jones (1993: 24) stated, "One of the great, old genealogical maxims is 'Cite your sources,'" so he reported every story as it was given to him, each with "the name of a prominent family historian attached to it as its author." Though Jones said he was fully aware of the stigma associated with the psychic, he found the possibility of intuition and coincidence playing a part in genealogy research irresistible. He writes that by and large, his apprehensions were unwarranted. "Most all of my responses suggested that I really had tuned into something!"

As Jones (1993: 24) collected the stories that were mailed to him, he wondered "if there might be some sort of commonality to the experiences" and began arranging them in categories "trying to see if any patterns of type or frequency might emerge. I also made careful record of my colleagues' views as to why they thought these phenomena might be happening." Several themes became apparent and formed the chapters of Jones' *Psychic Roots* books.

I have identified several characteristics from his interview and the collected memorates helpful for a folkloric discussion:

The 'cemetery stumble': This is my term for the 'urban legend' of tripping on the sought-after gravestone among hundreds. "I have had people on my radio shows tell me they have walked into large cemeteries and gone straight to the graves of their ancestors, even though they had never been there previously," wrote Nick Vine Hall of Australia (Jones, 1993: 29).

Coincidences of timing: "For many years I have experienced a phenomenon I am totally unable to explain. I will get a letter from one part of the country with Rose family information. Then within a day or two (sometimes even on the same day) I will get a letter or phone call from another part of the country requesting information on that same Rose group. This happens often." Christine Rose (Jones, 1993: 86).

Unexpected finds: Sought-after information turning up where it should not be, e.g. the librarian providing the wrong microfiche or the wrong book, which in fact had the sought-after names.

Feelings of Déjà vu: A deeply moving sense of homecoming when visiting ancestral sites.

Intuition and hunches: "Sometimes a hunch can be the gentlest and simplest of nudges to look in a particular place or do something a certain way" (Jones 1993:128). "As a normal rule, I don't peruse periodicals if they don't have an index, but in this one instance, I did. I can't say why I checked those few issues that we received in our library page-by-page. It was just one of those hunches that you get. It is hard to believe that, out of those few periodicals, they would contain just the clue I needed to help me find my Potters and Stewarts in Ireland!" Mary A. Pitts (Jones, 1993: 129).

Feeling led, guided, or pushed: These are random urges to look at something not on one's agenda. "On numerous occasions I have been doing research, and on an impulse, I would take a book from the shelves and open it up to find information on the families I was working on." Lahoma Lindeman of Layton, Utah (Jones 1993: 41). "I felt I was being 'pushed' to that book." Dr W. Cary

Anderson of Decatur, Arkansas (Jones, 1993: 41). "'Something' prompted me to check the book page by page." Dorothy M. of Lower of Fort Wayne Indiana (Jones, 1993: 42).

Serendipity: This term used by Jones has been picked up by genealogists. 'Serendipity' is a word taken from *The Three Princes of Serendip* by Horace Walpole (1717-1797). The traveling princes always came upon "by chance of sagacity, goals that they were not in quest of" (Jones, 1993).

Dreams: At times, Jones dreamed of the Palatine immigrants coming to redirect him when he was looking in the wrong place. Respondents described similar happenings: "I found myself dreaming about Bethia, and she haunted my thoughts by day. I would be in that 'twilight zone' just before falling asleep, and her name would just repeat itself over and over in my brain. Finally, I said out loud, 'OK Bethia, if you're trying to tell me something, I'll look into your family.'" Joanne Wharfield Roberts of Miami, Florida (Jones, 1997: 144).

Seeking meaning: "I felt sort of freaked out and bemused over this strange coincidence: what could be the 'significance' of this happening, if any? Now why in the world did I flip open to just that page, and why in the world did I stop to read it! [...] I have no logical explanation – other than serendipity – or magic! This type of coincidence used to unsettle me, but now I take it as a common, everyday experience" (Jones 1993: 86).

Feeling loved, hugged: Jones shyly admitted, "If they (the feelings) are really outlandishly spooky, I feel I'm getting a hug" (Jones, Interview 2012).

Sense of being chosen: Jones felt compelled to do the research – that he was a "conduit" for the ancestors.

The ancestors are helping: This involves the sense that the ancestors want to be found. This interesting concept will be discussed further when I propose the genealogist's work as a liminal, bridge function paralleling the role of a shaman.

The above categories illustrate examples of genealogists' experiences that form distinct classes with stable perceptual patterns. The experiences occur independently of their prior beliefs, knowledge, or intention. These are what Hufford (1995: 28) calls "core experiences" in his experiential source theory. The lore of paragenealogy is transmitted informally, orally, and through personal communication by letters or the Internet. It is stable in that certain themes recur and is dynamic in that the themes are told with variations by each percipient.

After initial warm-up questions, the interview picked up energy as Jones slipped with practiced ease into his role of speaker at a seminar. He told his story of becoming interested in genealogy as a boy and how he began to feel a supernatural connection with the Palatines during his research. The anecdotes he related were well-rehearsed, and I recognized most of them as they appear almost verbatim in his books. For this reason I found that asking about the experiences met a somewhat fixed stance, as if he had already decided what he thought. Fresh feelings and insights were initially not very accessible, but this changed as the interview progressed.

The interview brought up information that I did not recall having read in his books: for example, the strong, positive set of emotions he has about working with the supernatural and the significance of the experiences, not just for him but for everyone, not just the genealogy community, but all human beings. The emotional content arose when I pointed out that I did not remember reading that people spoke of 'feeling loved' and 'crying' when they came to an ancestor's home. Jones said he did not put that in his publications for fear of being "too syrupy." I inquired further,

[149]

"When you have one of those 'findings' after following a hunch, do you get a feeling of something different, a tingling or presence?"

"I get a feeling, yes. I know what you're asking. I get a feeling that whatever it is I'm doing is, 'You're on the right track.' It's a very subtle, warm reinforcement, and it tells me to keep going. Plus sometimes if they're really outlandishly spooky, I feel I'm getting a hug" (Jones, Interview 2012). Jones expressed a delight and awe as he spoke, suggesting he has had a peak spiritual experience.

In spite of a "strong Methodist" upbringing, Jones believes that his thinking was tempered by his mother's open-mindedness and by a grandmother who was respected for her psychic gifts. Later, he had a career in film and music in Hollywood where he was exposed to many unusual people and ideas. A medium once told Jones he may be a reincarnation of one of the Palatines, come back to finish something. He said it was interesting, but he was not sure about accepting this idea.

Jones has, over time, developed a voice to speak about his belief in the reality of supernatural events in genealogical research and in other areas of his life. His upbringing would not have supported that, nor would the professional genealogical societies. As he shared his paranormal stories and saw the floodgates open with the reports that came in to him, he "felt supported," "affirmed," and "reinforced." He has gone from feeling "weird" and "timid" to gradually increasing confidence that his experiences are not only real but positive. Jones thanked me for approaching him for the interview, voicing the following, "I hadn't read my books in ten years. I mean, I use some of my favourite stories in my seminars, but I hadn't read the books. And it (re-reading them) was a wonderful reinforcement of their acceptance. And that I was on the right track" (Jones, Interview 2012).

We can say that Jones uncovered a subculture of believers in the supernatural within the non-believing majority in the profession. Fears and guardedness about speaking of the supernatural are reported by the genealogists who responded, as well as Jones (1993: 21), who was at the outset "somewhat timid" about publicly mentioning his unusual experiences, unsure about how he would be received, "preparing myself for the possibility of ridicule." Jones' comments are consistent is consistent with the defensive reaction my initial queries met with during the research. The supernatural is still unstable ground in American culture. The authority of the professional genealogist's organization is a looming umbrella, so believers keep to themselves any non-logical experiences not supported by current scientific methods. Jones refers to fear of "the butterfly net," that is, being labeled crazy and thereby having one's work discredited:

> I always tried to make it clear to my colleagues that in no way was I trying to negate or minimize the proven and logical 'scientific approach' to genealogy, as championed by the late Donald L. Jacobus and my fellow Fellows of the American Society of Genealogists. Their emphasis on thorough documentation and the careful weighing of evidence in constructing a family pedigree will always be inviolate in my view (Jones, 1993: 20).

This comment, underlining the power of authority in genealogy and the dominant culture that brings cautionary behaviour to the percipients of supernatural events. "Official structures involve power, official belief operates with access to greater power and therefore to resources, than does folk belief" (Hufford, 1995: 23). The official structures, such as the American Association of Professional Genealogists, determine credibility.

Seeking meaning and questioning the experience was common in the responses of the genealogists: 'Why did this happen? What did it mean?' This reaction echoes the findings of Virtanen in *That Must Have Been ESP: An Examination of Psychic Experiences*. Virtanen comments on "unexplained experiences" in her Finnish sample of 135 respondents. Many voiced comments similar to the following: "This experience has been on my mind for years, and I wanted to tell it to someone, but who believes that we are surrounded by a spirit world?" (Virtanen, 1977: 136).

Certain terms have become part of the 'specialized vocabulary' used for discussing paranormal genealogy. Frequently genealogists report looking in the 'wrong place', such as the wrong microfilm or a book that falls to the floor, and coincidentally finding what they sought. 'Serendipity' has become a safe word for genealogists to use. Bennett (1995: 125) similarly reports a study of elderly women in a neighborhood using specifically charged words to talk about their psychic gifts. This 'specialized vocabulary' or 'vernacular' became evident as Jones began to collect stories. In *Psychic Roots*, he noticed the recurrence of certain phrases and words, such as: *serendipity, synchronicity, coincidence, intuition, a hunch, small world, being led, met the right person at the right time, lucky, stumbled over a crucial name or date,* and *it's all in the timing*. Also, buzzwords occur, such as, *uncanny, weird, spooky, feeling loved,* and what Jones deems most important, the concept that "*the ancestors want to be found*." Another descriptive phrase genealogists use that Jones delightedly told me about is the neologism "*having a Hank Jones moment*." This light-hearted phrase, referring to Jones' interest in the supernatural is used for any unexpected or uncanny occurrence while doing research.

The terminology used by genealogists to discuss the psychic events is fairly consistent and meaningful within the believers' subculture of genealogy. Jones (Interview, 2012) said, "I realized that some people don't have the words to say what they're feeling about the area. Also they wanted a safe place to talk about this. They needed a safe place to talk about it where they wouldn't get ridiculed."

The publication of Jones' first book not only provided a forum and support for those who had these experiences but also normalized the way people referred to their experiences, using this specialized vocabulary. The acceptance of paranormal experiences by genealogists, many of whom declare that they had no previous belief, knowledge, or intention to have supernatural experiences in their prior world-view, fits a defining characteristic of Hufford's (1995: 28) experiential source theory as described in 'Beings without Bodies'. Hufford's theory has three points, each of which may be considered against the data provided in Jones's collected narratives and his own experiences.

Firstly, *many widespread spiritual beliefs are supported by experiences that refer intuitively to spirits without reference or retrospective interpretation,* and secondly, *these occur independently of a subject's prior beliefs, knowledge, or intention.* Most percipients who responded to Jones's survey reported being taken by surprise. The genealogists, by and large, were taken unexpectedly by the strange, other-worldly sweetness of finding information where it should not have been. They were able to incorporate the strangeness into their personal worldview, no matter what that was, but typically withheld the telling of the story. And thirdly, *such experiences provide a central empirical foundation from which some supernatural beliefs develop naturally.* The perceived reality of the genealogists' experiences has led to belief in possibilities of supernatural intervention not considered previously. For Jones, the belief has become a conviction that the ancestors want to be found. Jones (Interview, 2012) says, "It is an evolving situation. I find that the mainstream is changing. You're going to find so many people are now more open." Asked if he thought the media had something to do with the changes, the increase in openness, he replied:

I think that people are just more exposed to stuff, just general stuff. One of the biggest (changes) in genealogy is the Internet because there's so much garbage out there. Like, people read the *National Inquirer* at the supermarket every week and say, 'Well, if it's in print, it's gotta be true.' And they're saying that about the Internet now, and that's our biggest albatross in genealogy right now. I think people are not getting together as much anymore (Jones, Interview, 2012).

Leea Virtanen similarly laments the loss that technology has brought to folklore of the supernatural, as technology impacts face-to-face gatherings. She writes:

Folk narration could be divided into two eras: the period before the advent of television and the period thereafter. Industrialism saw the end of quiet nights without electricity, people gathered by the fire, and as people stopped making clothes and tools in a self-sufficient economy, the folklore that accompanied handwork lost its place. The television took away the time and energy previously used for folk narration. Thus the ghost tales and speculation on the meaning of such supernatural experiences disappeared (Virtanen 1992: 229).

Jones likewise expressed mixed feelings about modern technology and using the Internet as a resource and forum for genealogical research. It offers attractive software for genealogists, so that working at home in solitude is more common than the former trips to libraries, archives, and town halls. Concerned about the increased number of errors in genealogy research that occurs in solitary Internet work, he asserts, "They are getting it wrong." There is reduced opportunity for interaction with others in the field, less chance for the serendipitous chance meeting with a stranger in a library, archive, or graveyard, whose story is linked with yours, and for the building-up of community and the sharing of stories. "They miss all the fun," Jones laments. The community created by genealogical research has been important to him, just as community is to the nature of folklore.

Spirituality is an important topic that Jones and the respondents return to repeatedly. The meaning of the experiences can often be discounted as coincidence, but the comments suggest that a sense of purpose is connected to the events, placing the paranormal anomalies in a theological framework if Belden Lane's four axioms for spiritual experience is applied. Jones felt compelled to do this research, as if he were a conduit. Genealogists feel 'led' or 'guided', thus:

The experience is not chosen; rather, it chooses: The experiences happen to the genealogists on an ordinary plane, as in libraries, or online. They claim no prior mind-set or expectations, thus:

The experiences are unexpected, unsought: The ancestry researcher's paranormal experiences create surprise, a 'letting go' of presuppositions. There is no intention entry into the moment of the experience. It just happens, thus:

The experience can be tread upon without being entered: The percipients report feeling personal meaning inwardly and connection to all the ancestors and the living community, outwardly, thus:

The experience is both centrifugal and centripetal: These four characteristics allow designation of some of the percipients' experiences as perceived as spiritual. In addition, there is a perception of a greater purpose, a connection to the dead and the living. There is a sense of helping the deceased, as well as helping the descendants. A Miami genealogist writes:

Our ancestors want to be found. In a sense what we're doing isn't about genealogy at all. It's really about our own journey and our own lessons learned. It is about feeling about one's ancestors, as well thinking about them, finding out more about them. It helps them; it helps everybody. Everybody wins." Joanne Wharfield Roberts of Miami, Florida. (Jones, 1997: 144).

The paranormal experiences seem to encourage, comfort, and provide the feeling of a guiding presence and connectedness to a larger community, both living and dead, especially noticed when immersed in solitary research. Genealogists who spend time and energy on the threshold between the living and the dead focus on information that strengthens relations among the living. A cognitive framework with this intense focus engenders a sense of relationship with the dead. Another perspective, drawing now from my own prior training as a Depth Psychologist could offer some insight into the way the percipients interpret their relationship with the dead. Genealogists typically spend long hours in graveyards, places that evoke the world of the departed, in a state of 'liminality' a threshold described in 'The Liminal Period in Rites of Passage' by anthropologist Victor Turner (1987: 7), who in turn drew on the theories of Arnold van Gennep.

Genealogists move between the two stages of life and death, this world and the next. These researchers describe feeling disorientation in the face of overwhelming information, as the paranormal experiences may be associated with a state of altered consciousness. This may happen inadvertently when there is a lowering of the conscious defenses, as the fatigued state that ensues from hours in archives and on a computer.

Liminality, the term for a state of transition between two realities or states of being may describe the somewhat altered state of mind of the fatigued and isolated genealogist who is focused on the deceased. The parallel role of the shaman, "who travels to the land of the dead communicating with the ancestors and returning with instructions" (Steadman & Palmer, 1994: 181) is arguably mimicked by genealogists who become recipients of supernatural communication in an almost quasi-shamanic role.

Several of the genealogists' stories illustrate that they believe that the ancestors have a vested interest in being found and remembered. The ancestors are also concerned about the well-being of living descendants. Some interesting insights may be suggested in a parallel to the genealogists' role in the greater society by looking at studies of ancestor worship. Benefits of ancestor worship include the creation of kinship and community. This recalls the genealogists' feeling of being pulled towards connected to others both living and deceased. Dead ancestors in traditional religions are, "not typically objects of worship, but methods of communication." (Steadman & Palmer, 1984: 181). Genealogist Ken D. Johnson, is cited in Jones' second volume, *More Psychic Roots* (1997), as saying, "It is my view that the dead sometimes invade our minds and guide us to the objects or documents we are seeking." Some of the genealogists surveyed described of using a sleep state to evoke an elusive ancestor. "Before I go to sleep at night, I 'program' myself to dream of a certain ancestor," writes Elaine Moss of Oconto, Wisconsin (Jones, 1997).

The Swiss psychiatrist Carl Jung theorized that when the consciousness is lowered, archetypal forms may emerge. In Jungian psychology, one could suggest that the images and sensations, dreams, and 'hunches' of the percipients may be effects of archetypal forms of the of the ancestors being activated in the genealogist's unconscious. Jung's autobiography, *Memories, Dreams, Reflections* (1961), describes his experiences during intentional states of liminal consciousness when he felt guided by images of spiritual figures and his deceased ancestors. "I feel very strongly that I am under the influence of things or questions which were left incomplete and unanswered by my parents and grandparents and more distant ancestors" (Jung 1961: 233). Interpretation is not the goal in this paper, but I introduce these ideas to include a broad and eclectic understanding of these reported experiences.

The genealogists' strange experiences do in fact quicken the pursuit of the ancestry research, pulling the seekers onwards and deeper into what otherwise could be just a compilation of dry names and dates. Virtanen (1977) writes:

> Informatory experiences are a remarkable feature of our culture. […] The standard world view prevalent in our society offers no places for such experiences. (Psychic) experiences open a door into a primal, subconscious stratum of the mind, a stratum that is otherwise out of reach.

The ancestry researchers surveyed describe their understanding of uncanny events that are remarkable in any culture, even cultures that accept and honour shamanic mediation between the living and the dead. The subculture of folk belief in supernatural experiences among genealogists is rich with informatory experiences that are shared guardedly. As a topic for folklore studies, para-genealogy is well-documented and continues to grow, as evidenced by unceasing letters to Jones, and in the para-genealogy websites that populate the Internet.

Summary
This concludes an overview on supernatural occurrences among genealogists. The proposal of this topic is appropriate for folkloric study in its consideration of the development of a sub-culture of paragenealogists within the larger framework of professional genealogy, and the "specialized vocabulary" vernacular described by Gillian Bennett (1995) that has developed among genealogists. There is a documented subculture of genealogists who believe in supernatural occurrences. This minority tends to set themselves apart from the dominant authority of non-believing, professional

genealogists. The percipients see themselves as needing a 'safe place' to share their stories. They have developed a specialized vocabulary. The stories are transmitted informally, orally or in letters, emails, and blogs. The psychic characteristics reported include coincidences, hunches, and dreams. There is a sub-belief that one is 'chosen' and that the deceased ancestors are helping and want to be found. The lore contained in oral narratives has stable content, even as the field evolves dynamically with use of the Internet and modern technology. Spiritual or quasi-shamanic states may be considered in describing the experiences, as percipients make connections with the deceased. The experiences are stable and may be described as what Hufford (1995: 28) calls "core experiences." That is, the experiences occur independently of their prior beliefs, knowledge, or intention as they occur outside the percipients' framework of belief.

There is food for thought in this topic regarding future research in folklore studies. The next level might include the following questions: Is status accrued in having and sharing the psychic experiences? Are there expectations, attempts at re-enactment of a paranormal experience? Is there an awareness or self-identification of liminal, altered consciousness or a quasi-shamanic role among genealogists? Of course, this is not an in-depth research study but represents a springboard for some fascinating discussions.

References

Bennett, G. 1995. If I Knew You Were Coming I'd Have Baked a Cake: The Folklore of Foreknowledge in a Neighborhood Group. In: B. Walker (Ed.), *Out of the Ordinary: Folklore and the Supernatural*. Logan: Utah State University Press, pp. 122-142.

Bradshaw, A. 2010. *True Miracles with Genealogy: Help from the Beyond*. Self-published.

Ellis, B. 2004. Visits to forbidden Graveyards. In: *Lucifer Ascending: The Occult in Folklore and Popular Culture*. Lexington: University Press of Kentucky, pp. 112-141.

Gallup Poll. 2005. (www.gallup.com/poll/.../three-four-americans-believe-paranormal) accessed 22 July 2014.

Hufford, D.J. 1995. Beings Without Bodies. In: B. Walker (Ed.), *Out of the Ordinary: Folklore and the Supernatural*. Logan: Utah State University Press, pp. 11-45.

Jones, H.Z. Jr. 1993. *Psychic Roots: Serendipity & Intuition in Genealogy*. Baltimore: Genealogical Publishing.

Jones, H.Z. Jr. 1997. *More Psychic Roots: Further Adventures in Serendipity & Intuition in Genealogy*. Baltimore: Genealogical Publishing.

Jung, C.G. 1961. *Memories, Dreams, Reflections*. R. Winston (Transl.). New York: Vintage.

Lane, B.C. [1998] 2002. *Landscapes of the Sacred: Geography and Narrative in American Spirituality*. Baltimore: Johns Hopkins.

Steadman, L.B. & Palmer, C.T. 1994. Visiting Dead Ancestors: Shamans as Interpreters of Religious Traditions. In: *Zygon* 29 (2), pp. 173-189.

Turner, V.W. 1987. The Liminal Period in Rites of Passage. In: L.C. Mahdi et al. (Eds.), *Betwixt & Between: Patterns of Masculine and Feminine Initiation*. La Salle, IL: Open Court, pp. 3-19.

Van Gennep, A. [1908]1960. *The Rites of Passage*. M. B. Vizedom & G. L. Caffee (Transl.). Chicago: University of Chicago Press.

Virtanen, L. 1977. '*That Must Have Been ESP': An Examination of Psychic Experiences*. J. Atkinson & T. DuBois (Transl.). Bloomington: University of Indiana.

Virtanen, L. 1992. Have Ghosts vanished with Industrialism? In: *Folklore Processed: In Honour of Lauri Honko on this 60th Birthday 6 March 1992* (Studia Fennica Folkloristica, 1), Helsinki: Suomalaisen Kirjallsuuude Seura.

Chapter 7

Traits of Transmission and Preservation: Interpreting Digital Versions of Folktales and Folk Songs from India

Tulika Chandra
Shiv Nadar University, India

Introduction

The oral tradition or 'Shruti' in India can be traced back to ancient times, when folklore was seen as source of entertainment and a means of communicating values. With the transition of text, context, linguistic aspects, tradition, culture, and beliefs, the folktales are effortlessly passed on from one generation to the next. Most of the folktales are communicated orally as the common folk practice orality to relate their pasts. This paper focuses on the interpretation of folklore and its link value systems. The empirical work from Braj, a region in the northern Indian state of Uttar Pradesh, is used as the basis for a case study to enrich understanding of transmission traits through folktales and folk songs.

The paper is structured as follows: The first section introduces the folk tradition in India, in particular describing orality as a medium; the 'folk' as the narrators of the tales; and the geographical area that provides the study's context. The section also deliberates upon the scholarly work of experts in the domain, followed by a brief overview of the theory of active and passive tradition bearers by the folkloristic theoretician Carl Wilhelm von Sydow (1948). The next section, which is the core of the study, discusses the role of the individuals who perform the folklore and the purpose of these performance, entailing the cultural and social perspective associated with the traits of folklore transmission and preservation. The last section consists of concluding remarks.

Folktales and the associated landscape
This paper considers the genres, folktales, and folk songs of a small but significant region, popularly known as Braj, in northern India. While interpreting these genres, the 'narrator' as well as the 'narrative' are also considered. Orality or 'Shruti' does not distinguish the elite from the folk and is not restricted to certain communities, classes, castes, or religions.

Folktales and folk songs are integral to Braj or 'Braj Bhoomi'. The ancient texts, epics, and folklore within this region create culturally (though not politically) defined borders and demarcations, so that Braj can be said to cover an area of approximately 5000 km^2. Mentioned as a political state in the epic Mahabharata, Braj is believed to be the birth place of the Hindu deity Krishna and 'witness' to his childhood and adolescence, site of Krishna's mischievous pranks, magnetism, charisma, and extraordinary heroic acts. According to the 'Braj Foundation' it is estimated that around 50 million pilgrims and tourists visit Braj annually. The folktales and folk songs draw their existence from religion; region; rituals; festivals; interactions with humans, with demons, and evil spirits; etc. Most of the folktales and folk songs are experiences based on incidental events, but they impart considerable moral and social knowledge.

The 'folk', as Alan Dundes (1980: 6) defines the term, is a group of people who share at least one common linking factor. The natives or the folk of Braj, popularly known as Brajwasi, are passionate about and are possessive of their folklore. They view folklore as 'their own heritage', their history, and 'events that have occurred in the place to which they belong'. The older generation can be seen as the direct medium between the narrator and the listener and are involved in transmitting folklore to the next generation. The transmission has occurred in unbroken succession from ancient times to the present day. Each narration and each folk song has the echo, vivacity, liveliness, and vibration of an actual human voice. The languages mainly spoken are 'Braj bhasha' and Hindi, which belong to the Indo-Aryan family of languages.

Yeats (1888) has stated the importance of folklore for all who are in the area of literature and states: "No conscious invention can take the place of tradition, for he who would write a folktale, and thereby bring a new life into literature must have the fatigue of the spade in his hands and the stupors of the fields in his hearts." Folklorists who believe in collecting folklore have the massive task of entering into the field and collecting data, rendering accuracy imperative. The video recordings of folk-narratives that the author gathered from the Braj region were minimally edited, and no attempt was made to make changes in the name of preservation or interpretation.

Eminent folklorists like Aarne and Thompson as well as Propp have analysed folktales and other folk genres. Structural analysis conducted by Propp (1968) takes the morphology of the folkloristic text into account, and the text is described by considering the chronological order of the linear sequence of elements – one sequence followed by another – as 'told' by the consultant/informant. Some other scholars have analysed the text, based on syntactic analysis, in which the 'given order' is broken and regrouped in an analytical schema. Propp's structural analysis is undoubtedly remarkable, but it fails to relate folklore to culture, and the analysis is best suited to 'fairy tales'. Folklore, however, is not only about fairy tales and cannot be divorced from culture and tradition.

Involving entities for meaningful interpretation
Sydow (1948) advocated the concept of 'oicotype' and suggested that folktales and other genres of folklore – like plants – become accustomed to specific surroundings through natural selection and thus differ somewhat from other members of the same species, in this case general tale-types. For Sydow (1948), "It is not enough to study folktales as tales only. It is also necessary to make oneself familiar with the use of folk-tales, their life in tradition, their transmission and spread." Folktales from Braj are reused and renewed by the narrators as they respond to their cultural surroundings.

While discussing the folklore, we must credit the folk of Braj as performers and partners. They must be noted while documenting, collecting, classifying, and cataloguing the information and interpretations that they provide concerning the folklore. The informants' involvement leads us to observe the present-day realities of cultural forms and processes so that we can understand the insiders' perspective on discourse and practice, which allows us to appreciate the people and their culture. A wealth of empirical data has been collected from the region. But how should we categorise these 'folk' who provide data? Do we identify them as 'informants', or do we categorise them as 'consultants'? The folktales and folk songs are recorded in constant contact with the people, so they cannot be simply termed 'sources'. They are instead a helpful group who contribute as equals in understanding and analysing the material. They can be easily termed 'consultants', who are involved in sharing information. These consultants need to be appreciated for their cooperation and willingness to share their narratives. They have been involved not only in transmission but have also contributed immensely towards preserving the folklore.

Interpretations of these folktales illustrate how changes and revisions are part of the form of their retelling. The basic outline of the folktale or the song is preserved by the narrator/ performer while she/he incorporates new traditions into the story or the song. The art of narrating is carried out effectively by the folk, who convey specific regional, religious, cultural, and knowledge aspects of the folktales with exceptional precision. The narrator is constantly linking the present to the past. When discussing forms of narration, the notion of 'normal form' must be taken into account. Georges and Owens (1995: 128) have stated, "Whatever the expansion, subdivision, merger, or redefinition of the type set, there still exists the notion of what the past is or should be. This concept is the *normalform*. It lies at the basis of configuring phenomena into type sets in folkloristics." The 'normalform' is similar to what we have as preserving the outline of the narrative. Folktale narrators from Braj preserve the outline of the narrative: The tales begin with varied introductions, move ahead by narrating the exploits of the characters, and usually end on a happy note.

The collected tales were classified by their means of oral narration, following Propp's assertion that "Since the tale is exceptionally diverse and evidently cannot be studied at once in its full extent, the material must be divided into sections i.e. it must be classified. [...] The accuracy of all further study depends upon the accuracy of classification" (Propp, 1968: 5).

Influencing factors: Active and passive bearers
Carl von Sydow (1948) suggests that folklore, transmitted "through the human bearers of tradition," from one individual to another, depends on two kinds of tradition bearers: active tradition bearers

and passive tradition bearers. From this perspective, 'active tradition bearers' are individuals in a community who actually narrate or perform the tales or songs. Passive tradition bearers are the audience who carry the tradition with them to other places. Von Sydow's distinction can be applied to transmission of the folklore genres narrated and performed in Braj. The active tradition bearers in Braj are the folk, cutting across all classes, castes, regions, and religions – whether an 'elite' from the Brahmin caste, a woman sitting outside the temple guarding shoes, a humble farmer, a tourist guide or educated young person.

The art of narrating the folktales is impacted by various factors. An important factor in the Braj region is its popularity as a pilgrimage destination for domestic tourists from the Indian subcontinent. Tourism has helped keep folktales and folk songs 'alive', though changes are evident in their language and content. Use of new technology also makes an impact. Narrative style is influenced by the languages currently being spoken in the area, resulting in more dramatized and customized forms of narration.

When interpreting folktales and folk songs we must take the narrators into account, giving equal importance to active and passive tradition bearers. In Braj, active bearers are proud of their past and their heritage and have a motive for carrying out the transmission, yet passive bearers are eager and enthusiastic carriers of tradition as well. During the fieldwork, when the consultants were asked permission to shoot the video recordings, they were not at all camera conscious, rather all of the consultants were more than happy to get their story or song to be recorded. They were not bothered about their physical appearance, their surroundings, or their clothes and were eager to narrate whatever they had heard from older generations. Besides being active tradition bearers, most narrators must actively make a living. Their major source of income is domestic tourists. The 'oicotype' here involves specific folktale patterns that are popular with a particular social groups in a particular geographic region.

Passive tradition bearers can be categorized into two groups: those who feel nostalgic for the past and those who feel the impulse to do 'something', for instance a compulsion to record or detail the region's existing uniqueness. Active tradition bearers, on the other hand, are categorized through the position of a few questions in light of interpretations of folktales and folk songs. The questions posed are:

(I) Individuals involved in performing the folklore: Who is the narrator/performer? What is the purpose behind narration/performance, i.e. why is the folklore performed/ narrated?

(II) Cultural and social perspective: Bearing in mind the cultural context, are the songs or tales designed to inform? To teach? To suggest moral and ethical ideals? To warn? To validate something? Or simply to entertain?

Interpreting the folktales and folk songs from the first perspective (i.e. from I) leads to the categorization of active tradition bearers, encompassing (A) local common people engaged in livelihoods as farmers, merchants, petty shopkeepers, housewives, government employees, and the like as well as (B) local people involved directly in providing varied services to the tourists.

Narrators in the first category (A) are proud Brajwasis, for whom folktales and folk songs are a means of expressing belief, love, imagination, devotion, and adoration. This category of folk identifies itself with these tales and songs. Their tales and songs revolve around the 'Hero'. Their tales often narrate the supernatural exploits of the Hindu deity Krishna, legendary incidents in which the hero annihilates the villain. Most of the narratives have a humble beginning by introducing the 'hero' besides prominently including the region in the narration, develop with the acts, and end with a moral. The performers celebrate, rejoice, pray, or express fear through the folktales or folk songs. Braj is vibrant with performers belonging to all age groups, with certain similarities and differences among the various age groups. In our fieldwork, the older generation (45+ years old) and children (6–14 years old) proved to be energetic and happy performers, making use of a wealth of expressions. The middle age group, consisting of younger adults, is more thoroughly exposed to 'Bollywood' (popular Hindi cinema/ Indian film industry) and television and shows more interest in 'filmi' (film) songs and movies at the local cinema. This young generation is generally less interested in performing and narrating. There may be multiple reasons for this, including the increasing number of educated youths, improved possibilities for commuting to larger cities, contact with tourists, and easy internet access.

Influencing factors: Tourists
A large number of tourists, both domestic and international, flock to the Braj region every year. Pilgrims and tourists from the other Indian states come as domestic tourists to the places like Mathura, Vrindaban, Barsana, Chhata, and Gokul. International tourists also visit Braj towns, such as Agra, the city of the Taj Mahal or Vrindaban.

The second category of active tradition bearers (B) consists of locals who are directly involved in providing services to tourists. They have a definite identity as narrators or performers. Their tales narrate the significance of a particular place and focus on heroic deeds or supernatural adventures, ending with the 'victory of good over evil'. These narrators, who are proud to be Brajwasis, use folklore not only as a means of expressing belief but also as a way of making a living. They view domestic tourists as their source of income. This second category (B) can furthermore be subdivided into three groups:

[168]

(i) The priests (Goswamis or Pandits), who work for the various pilgrimage sites (small, medium, or large temples) or other historical sites

(ii) Tourist guides

(iii) Other facilitators.

Priests, Pandits, or Goswamis (i) belong to the Brahmin caste, and most belong to families that have been associated with a pilgrimage site or a particular temple for several generations. Tales and songs have been passed on from generation to generation by their ancestors in speech or writing. Since domestic tourists interact with them directly, they are in a way the most prominent group of tradition bearers. They are the ones who narrate the folktales associated with a particular site. The characters of these folktales and songs are taken usually from the *Gita, Shrimad Bhagavad,* or *Mahabharata* religious epics.

Apart from the folktales taken from the epics, many other folktales are also narrated, sometimes to attract, warn, inform, or even scare the visitors for the sake of making earning income from them. The same person may retell the same folktales many times a day. These orally narrated folktales are more or less the same as are used by all three of the socio-economic classes: rich Goswamis (priests), middle-income Goswamis, and economically weaker Goswamis. The 'elite' and 'educated' Goswamis avoid interactions with general tourists while the other two groups make a living by directly interacting and communicating with the visitors and tourists, who are mostly devotees. These priestly narrators belong to all age groups and get involved in the profession at a very young age, sometimes as young as eight or nine years old. These young folklore narrators possess excellent narrative styles. Women are not encouraged to become priests; this is an all-male domain.

(ii) Apart from the priests, the other prominent group of active tradition bearers in Braj consists of tourist guides. Tourist guides narrate the same folktales (only very occasionally folk songs) as the Goswamis. They may belong to the Brahmin community or be from any other caste or community. Tourist guides in Braj operate privately, and there are very few government-approved guides. Folktales narrated by these tourist guides are mostly ones that have been learned or heard from the Goswamis. These tales are told, retold, and reconstructed many times in order to validate any narrative example or any historic or pilgrimage site. Narration of the folktales begins with an introduction to the place. The hero (protagonist) is often from the place in question, and the tale ends with focus on the victory of the local 'hero'. The hero in these tales is not gender discriminated. These tourist guides are convincing, persuasive, effective teller of tales and are well versed in the art of narration. Tourist guides may belong to any age group, and the fieldwork found guides as young as eight or nine years of age and as old as 92.

(iii) The third category under (B) comprises natives of Braj, many of them are dependent on visitors and tourists to earn their living. They also cater to the needs of the local population. This category also has a wealth of folktales and folk songs, which they perform at various functions on different occasions. Folktales narrated by them are full of life, with numerous illustrative details. Folk songs sung by them have lyrics that dramatize an incident or heroic act or glorify an occasion. This is the group including people like the local halwai (sweets seller), shopkeepers, the dhaba-walas (small restaurant owners), handicraft artisans, musicians, tailors, sweepers, florists, rickshaw and auto-rickshaw drivers, boatmen, and the like. 'Professional' performers are also involved in making use of the folktales, making a living by performing varied folk-art forms like 'ras-leela' and 'nautanki'.

Folklore and the social as well as cultural perspective
We interpret our data from social and cultural perspectives. Folktales and folk songs are drawn from various societal dimensions. Regionality is one prominent spectrum of the folktales and folk songs, with geographical area making an impact on narration and performance as well as upon the beliefs themselves, the selection of legends, and the deities being worshipped. The folktales and folk song narrations are based upon mystical happenings and supernatural powers.

Narrated example of 'show of strength' (regional influence on folk narrative)
The fondly worshipped Hindu deities Radha and Krishna are at the centre of many of narratives. Radha is believed to have been brought up at Barsana (Braj), and Krishna is believed to have spent his later childhood days at Nandgaon (Braj), which is 8 km from Barsana. Radha is considered to be Krishna's 'Shakti' (strength). One folktale gives the story of young Krishna at a place known as Gowardhan, where he held up Giriraj Hill on the tip of his little finger continuously for seven days and seven nights to shield the Brajwasi (people of Braj) from a deluge of rains sent down by Indra (another Hindu deity). At Barsana, the same folktale narrates the same incident but also includes the element that Radha helped Krishna hold up Giriraj Hill by holding it with her eyelashes.

Narrated example of 'Incarnation'
In another folktale, the Hindu deity Shiva shows his desire to visit and meet the infant Krishna, who was born as a normal human being on earth. The tales and songs express this event as one Avtaar (incarnation) meeting another Avtaar on earth. Krishna's mother is apprehensive about Shiva's appearance (Shiva is believed to have snakes around his neck, his hair tied in a bun atop his head) and thus prevents his entry into the house. Shiva waits outside the house

until Kanha (another name for Krishna) cries and wails to let Shiva in. This folktale is narrated in the same structure at two different places, both Nandgaon and Gokul, where Krishna is believed to have spent his early childhood days. The distance by road between the two towns is approximately 54 km.

Narrated example of 'good conquering evil'
Legendary characters from the Mahabharata and Dhola Nal epics also appear in the folk narratives. The tales and the songs are about prosperity and how their 'hero' reclaims a lost empire by conquering a demon. Legendary figures like Vrishbhan, Dauji, Ashwasthama, Kansa, and Agrasen make an impact in the folktales and songs. The 'folk' have an immeasurable connection to these characters. Tales are narrated in praise of the King of Braj Bhoomi, the local hero Vrishbhan. Vrishbhan is Radha's father, and the Rawalgaon area has a number of folktales that glorify his might and powers.

Another example is of folktales from the small town of Baldev. Krishna's elder foster brother Dauji was believed to rule the estate of Baldev. Folk songs express him as symbol of prosperity and agriculture, and he is believed to be a 'God of the Farmers', who is soft-spoken and patient. Folktales related to Dauji in and around the town of Baldev narrate his brave exploits: They portray him as involved in defeating and destroying demons and evil powers with support from Krishna. Yet another example is of Ashwasthama, another legendary character from the epic Mahabharata. He is believed by the natives to still be alive and is awaiting salvation. Each region, such as like Chhata, Barsana, and Dhola (all in Braj), has its own set of tales seeking to establish that Ashwasthama has been 'seen' near the jungles of the village/town.

These legendary characters are represented as 'superhuman', and folktales glorify their heroic and daring deeds and work as inspirational tales for the next generation. Folk songs are sung in their tribute, praise, and honour. Raja Nal, king of Dhola in Braj, is one such heroic characters, celebrated throughout Braj for having triumphed over his fate. Folk songs are sung in praise of Krishna at Barsana, who is worshipped not as a male but as a 'sakhi', a female friend of Radha at Ladliji Temple, Barsana.

Narrated example of 'eulogising women'
At Bharavali gaon, a small agrarian village in Braj, interpretation of the folk songs displays the unusual aspect of saluting and applauding great female characters from Braj's Hindu mythological texts and epics. The folk songs are sung by women, who hail the 'voice' of these female 'heroes'. They celebrate that these legendary female characters were the ones who managed to 'pull out' men when they were in trouble, with their strong willpower. The folk songs applaud Queen Tara, King Harish Chandra's wife. There are folk songs that salute Queen Draupadi's fight to save her chastity, virtue, and innocence all alone, who screams and seeks Krishna's help when none of her five strong husbands come forward to save her. Folk songs applause the act of Mother Kunti, who breaks the traditional norms and accepts and announces to the world that her eldest son was born out of wedlock. The tales and songs also salute the queens of Dhola and Durga for their courage in saving Raja Nal. Individuality, coupled with strength and determination to achieve justice and/or vengeance, forms the most common content of Braj folklore.

Narrated examples of 'religious sentiment' and 'festivities'
Religion plays a significant role in Braj folklore. The largest religious group in Braj Bhoomi are the Hindus, followed by Muslims, Sikhs, Christians, Jains, Buddhists, and tribal communities. Although each religion has its believers and followers, who are emotionally sensitive

and protective of their religion, the folktales and folk songs show the impact of 'region'. Agra, Fatehpur Sikri, and Mariyam's Tomb are the places with vibrant folklore. Agra is famous for the beautiful and immortal Taj Mahal, one of the world heritage sites.

Rituals, festivals, ceremonies are very important when we interpret Braj folklore. The folktales and songs are also seen as contributing to the formation of group identity and solidarity. Each ritual, festival, and ceremony is marked by a variety of tales and songs, which are narrated and sung in groups. While the folktales are simple narratives, folk songs have rich, striking forms such as the Rasiya, Rasleela, Hori, Jeekri, Sohar, and Barna-Barni. These folk songs are sung to celebrate marriage, child birth, festivals, and other occasions. Their contents and contexts differ, and their styles of presentation vary.

The folktales and songs celebrating festivals are actually narrated or sung on that particular day, in accordance with the religious calendar. One can speak of a folktale that expresses the importance of Karva Chauth, narrated by the 'suhagan' (married) women, who observe a fast for the entire day and sing folk songs, offering prayers for the prosperity, longevity, and wellbeing of their husbands. The folktales and songs voice the importance of celebrations for the next generation. Tales also suggest that Karva, or the earthen pot used in the festival, symbolizes wealth, prosperity, and prayers for good harvest.

Similar are the folktales and songs associated with Bhaidooj, a celebration that reinforces and rejoices the bond between brothers and sisters. The folktales narrate how, on Bhaidooj, a sister waits eagerly for her brother to come to her house so that she can pray for his wellbeing, and later in the tale, she fights and protects him from the evil, immoral, and the wicked.

Holi is a festival of colours that is celebrated for one day all across India. People splash water on each other and play with wet as well as dry colours (abeer-gulal). In Braj, this celebration of colours continues for 45 days at a stretch across the region. The Brajwasis call it Hori. The festivity is marked by various performances on each day. The folktales related to Holi narrate how Krishna, along with his friends known as 'gopi' and 'gopiyan', played Holi in Nandgaon and in Barsana: All of Braj is soaked colours, which is prominent in the forms of folk songs like 'Rasleela', 'Rasiya', and 'Hori'.

Lathmaar Holi is a very popular form of Holi celebrated at Barsana (believed to be Radha's birth place). The people of Barsana and Nandgaon re-enact whole scenes from the Radha and Krishna tales. The men belonging to Goswami (Brahmin) families from Nandgaon come to Barsana to play holi and accept 'lathh-maar' (getting hit by a long stick). Only married (suhagan) women who belong to Goswami sect can hit them with a beautifully decorated bamboo stick or 'lathh'. Only a chosen few can 'touch' or use these 'lathhs'. The 'lathmaar holi' begins at noon, with both the sides teasing each other through folk songs, singing 'Hori' and 'Rasiya'. This continues for around five hours. These are call-and-response folk songs. The verses that are exchanged are rich in content, primarily as verbal attacks in the form of questions and answers.

There are many other festivals and occasions concerning Krishna and Radha, such as Janmashtmi and Radha-ashtmi.

Narrated examples of the 'supernatural'
Folktales and folk songs are narrated to the next generation in all manner of places: in the paddy fields, at home, at temple, at school, at chaupal (open meeting place), while taking the cattle grazing. The younger generation, especially children aged 8-14, show interest in a particular type of folktale, those concerning the interactions between the supernatural, gods/goddesses, demons, devils, and evil spirits. The folktales are more popular in this respect

than are the folk songs. There are varied tales concerning the demons Hau–Bilau, Pootna, and Nakasur and how the supernatural powers of Krishna and Balram (Dauji) defeated and destroyed the evil forces. They all express belief in self and victory over evil as well as portray Krishna as saviour and protector of his folk. Krishna is believed to be an 'Avatar' (incarnation) with many stupendous powers, but at the same time, since he was born into the material world, so he plays all sorts of pranks and is naughty, like any normal child. This aspect is plays a dominant role in the folktales and folk songs.

Relating to and identifying with the past seems imperative for Brajwasis. This is how they relate to the folklore too. They see the folklore as 'my heritage', 'my history', 'my past', 'from my region'. The individual identifies herself/himself with the 'songs' and the 'tales' that are passed on from one generation to the next. The people's firm belief in supernatural powers allows these folktales to articulate the quintessence of the celestial, divine, blessed, superhuman, magical, mystical, and even the dark and evil. The folktales concerning instances of Krishna's or Radha's continued existence into the present day are narrated with excitement and enthusiasm. These folktales leave use to ponder over various questions, but the folk belief is so strong that these questions are not vocalized.

One of the folktales concerns how a small child, who frequently played the game of marbles alone in the lanes of Nandgaon town, was one day challenged to a game of marbles by an unfamiliar boy of his own age. This unfamiliar child (young Krishna) won all of the marbles, grabbed hold of them, and ran towards the Nandbaba temple (named after Krishna's father). The child from the town followed him to the temple, but by then this unfamiliar boy had disappeared. When the child from the town saw the idols, he identified the idol of young Krishna as the same boy who had been playing marbles with him, and the priest found some marbles lying near young Krishna's idol. Another tale relates how Radha, disguised as a pretty little girl, brought 'kheer' (rice pudding) for a hungry devotee and sage at Ted Kadam in Nandgaon town. At Mathura town, folktales show young Kanha guiding devotees who have taken the wrong parikrama path (circumambulation), playing pranks and scaring little girls, or helping his merchant devotee at Vrindaban by giving one of his bangles to clear merchant's debt.

Concluding remarks
The folktales and folk songs have an underlying meaning as well as a surface meaning. This underlying meaning may be regarded as metaphorical or symbolic, valuable as a general myth relevant to human nature and experience. This meaning is varied and unfathomable relative to the narrative's surface meaning.

Folktales and folk songs bear witness to the collective representation of the experiences of many generations. Their transmission automatically leads to preservation by the next generation. Efforts are ongoing to preserve these folktales and folk songs by publishing or digitally recording them. It is essential to create database to preserve this folklore in its present form through proper storage, observation, and study of the songs and tales that comprise it. The society is alive and dynamic. Because changes are natural and inevitable, now is the time to take steps to create digital versions of these folktales and folk songs in order to honour a particular time period and lay the foundations for comparative research into historical and contemporary narratives.

References
Chandra, T. 2013-2015. Active Project *Documentation of Folktales through Digitization*. Department of English. Shiv Nadar University.

Aarne, A., & Stith, T. (eds) 1981. *The Types of Folktales: A Classification and Bibliography*. Helsinki: Acadeia Scientiarum Fennica.

Dey, L.B. 1883. *Folktales of Bengal*. London: Macmillan

Dorson, R.M. (eds) 1972. *Folklore and Folklife*. University of Chicago Press.

Dorson, R.M. 1963. 'Current Folklore Theories', *Current Anthropology* 4(1).

Dundes, A. 1965. *The Study of Folklore*. Prentice Hall College Division.

Dundes, A. 1980. 'Interpreting Folklore'. Indiana University Press.

Dundes, A. (ed.) 1999. 'International Folkloristics: Classic Contributions by the Founders of Folklore'. Rowman & Littlefield.

Emeneau, M.B. 1989. 'Krsna Steals the Gopīs' Clothes: A Folktale Motif", *Journal of the American Oriental Society* 109(4).

Finneran, R.J., & Harper, G.M. (eds) 2010. *The Collected Works of W.B. Yeats Volume IX: Early Art: Uncollected Articles and Reviews Written Between 1886 and 1900*. Simon and Schuster

Frazer, J.G. 1922. *The Golden Bough A Study of Magic and Religion*. Brick Court, Temple, London.

Georges, R.A., & Jones, M.O. 1995. *Folkloristics: An Introduction*. Bloomington & Indianapolis: Indiana University Press.

Honko, L. 1964. 'Memorates and the Study of Folk Beliefs', *Journal of the Folklore Institute*, 1(1/2), 5-19.

Honko, L. 1998. *Textualising the Siri Epic*. Academia Scientiarum Fennica.

Levi-Strauss, C. 1976. *Structural Anthropology*. New York: Basic.

Ministry of Tourism, Government of India (2012) *Interim Report Uttar Pradesh 2012*. Parliament Street, Transport Bhawan, New Delhi.

Mournet, T.C. 2005. *Oral Tradition and Literary Dependency*. Mohr Siebeck.

Müller, M.F. 1881. *On the Migration of Fables*. Library of Alexandria.

Muiser, I.E.C., Theune, M., & Meder, T. 2012. 'Cleaning up and Standardizing a Folktale Corpus for Humanities Research'. University of Twente, Enschede, the Netherlands

Narayan, K. 1997. *Mondays on the Dark Night of the Moon: Himalayan Foothill Folktales*. Oxford University Press.

Naithani, S. 2009. *In Quest of Indian Folktales*. Orient BlackSwan.

Ranade, A.D. 2003. 'Traditional Musics and Composition in the Indian Context', *The World of Music, Traditional Music and Composition: For György Ligeti on His 80th Birthday* 45(2).

Propp, V. 1968. *Morphology of Folktales*. University of Texas Press.

Tagore, R.N. 1926. *An Indian Folk Religion*. Sir Rabindranath Tagore. Macmillan and Co, London.

Wolfram, W. 2007. *Sociolinguistic Folklore in the Study of African American English*. Blackwell.

Yeats, W.B. 1888. *Fairy and Folk Tales of the Irish Peasantry*, http://www.sacred-texts.com/neu/yeats/fip/. Edited and selected by W. B. Yeats. Accessed February 2014.

Von Sydow, C.W. 1948. *Selected Papers on Folklore*. Selected and edited by L. Bødker, Copenhagen.

Chapter 8

Carl Ferdinand Schertz's Legal Analysis of Vampirism

Giuseppe Maiello

Palacký University (Olomouc), Czech Republic

In 1872, the third chapter of Joseph Sheridan Le Fanu's novel *Carmilla* was published. Here, in the fictional library of the so-called Baron Vordenburg, the reader could find evidence of the *Magia posthuma*, a small book, written in 1703 by the Silesian writer Carl Ferdinand Schertz and published the following year.

The *Magia posthuma* is considered the most-quoted book on vampires in 18th-Century Western Europe (Introvigne, 1996: 20). This occurred thanks to the large number of quotations made in the mid-18th Century by Augustin Calmet, author of the most famous treatise on vampires and an inexhaustible source of information on vampires up until today. Calmet's book was original published in French in the year 1746 under the title *Dissertations sur les apparitions des anges, des démons et des esprits, et sur les revenants et vampires de Hongrie, de Bohême, de Moravie, et de Silésie* (Calmet, 1746). In English, it was known under the title *The Phantom World* (Calmet, 1850).

For many people interested in vampires, the *Magia posthuma* is simply a lost book. In the 'Vampire lovers' discussion on *goodreads.com*, we find for example, the following reader statement:

What I would give for a real copy of the Magia Posthuma. It was written for Prince Charles of Lorraine in 1706 and is a detailed account of the first serious investigations into vampire slayings. The Phantom World describes a couple of the most notorious cases from the Magia Posthuma. What a shame that the whole book is lost in the past (Cary, 2009).

The legend that the *Magia posthuma* is a lost or inaccessible book can also be found in modern literature, such as Prudence Foster's *Blood Legacy* (Foster, 2002: 209) and even in the scientific literature on vampires (see Pedersen, 2009: 13).

Despite less well-informed views, there are three copies of the *Magia posthuma* still preserved in the Czech Republic, including Karl Ferdinand Schertz's original manuscript, dated 1703. I worked with the copy preserved in the Manuscripts and Early Printed Books Department of the National Library of the Czech Republic in Prague and with the copy at the Silesian Muzeum in Opava. I saw a copy preserved in the Benedictine monastery of Rajhrad, near Brno, as well. Another copy surely also exists in France, at the *Bibliothèque municipale de Nancy*. That copy is probably the one that Augustin Calmet possessed when writing his dissertations on vampirism.

Like many books supposed lost, we find numerous legends connected with its author, the knight Carl Ferninand von Schertz (d. 1724), born in the village of Spalov, Silesia, now part of the Czech Republic in the Moravian-Silesian Region.

Here we seek to reconstruct the source of inspiration for Schertz's work devoted to *Spectri*, as the vampires were called in Latin before the year 1731, when the word 'vampire' started becoming common in European languages. 'Vampire' comes from a southern Slavic dialect, which is derived from the common Slavic word *upyr'*. Its etymology was definitively deciphered by the French linguist André Vaillant. The word *upyr'* originally meant 'he who escapes'

(Vaillant, 1931: 678), and it must thus be understood as a restless soul that moves away from the body after death or during sleep (see Maiello, 2004: 17). We have no problem using the term 'vampires' for all harmful living corpses and regarding the terms 'vampirism' and '*Magia posthuma*' as synonyms, to define the way in which the dead are supposed to appear in order to take the living with them to the afterlife. We also appreciate that similar conclusions were reached - through various routes - by other distinguished scholars, such as David Keyworth (2006) and Ármann Jakobsson. Jakobsson in particular refers to the great Scottish anthropologist Andrew Lang, when translating the Icelandic '*Draugr*' to 'Vampire' (Jakobsson, 2009: 307; Lang, 1897: 245).

Schertz based his study on three types of sources. The first type of source was the belief in vampires, which was very strong in the region which he came from; the second type consisted of historical records related to his region, the Czech-speaking part of the Silesia; and the third type was the rich literature on sorcery collected by writers from ancient Rome, ancient Greece, the Renaissance, and Baroque Europe.

According to Lubor Niederle (1916: 44), the first direct written reference to vampires in Central Europe dates to the year 745. Other written information on vampirism dates from the beginning of the 11th Century, for example the Burchard of Worms' Canon law. Among the items in this large collection of laws, we find such laws as the ban on impaling the corpses of the dead who are suspected of rising from their graves.

We do not know if Carl Ferdinand Schertz was aware of the two particular aforementioned sources, but we surely know that he was familiar with the oldest case of vampirism in Bohemia. This case was reported by Jan Neplach (1322-1371), abbot of the Benedictine monastery of Opatovice nad Labem, a village in the

Pardubice region, now in the Czech Republic. It was also reported by the chronicler Wenceslaus Hajek of Libočan (d. 1553) and finally by the Catholic historian Jan František Beckovský (1658-1722), who Carl Ferdinand Schertz considered to be the most authoritative source for the study of ancient Czech history.

According to Neplach, who was closest to the case chronologically, the first event took place in the year 1336 (but a more probable correct dating would have been 1334) in the village of Blov, in northwest Bohemia. Schertz first gives narrates the event to the reader, then gives his remarks. Here is Schertz's description:

In a village called Blov, about one mile from Kadaň, a certain shepherd called Myslata died and was buried at the church after a regular Christian funeral. Every night he rose and went into the surroundings, frightening and attacking people, and anyone who he called by name died in eight days. The inhabitants of the village and of the other villages in the area decided to dig him up and impale him with an oak spike, in the presence of them all. When he had been impaled, he seemed to smile and said: "Oh, you hurt me much, and you have also given me a staff to defend myself from the dogs." The very same night he rose again and frightened and attacked even more people than before. The inhabitants of the surroundings could suffer no more and therefore called for two hangmen and ordered them to dig him up and place him on a carriage. He was laid on his back, and they tied up half of his body with rope, when he bent his back like a living person, got up, and when they tied him up more he roared like the worst beast. Then they placed him on a pyre and tied stakes firmly to the ground, then one of the hangmen pierced him with an oak spike. Immediately he turned on his side, and blood poured out from him as if he was a beast. When the fire consumed him, he roared like a donkey.

After the cremation, all of the evil ceased (Schertz 1704; see Maiello 2014: 207-208).

As a lawyer interested in the complex issues regarding his region, Schertz analyses the account in detail, not only relative to the Catholic theology of his time but also in accordance with the rationalism of European jurisprudence.

In a village - First of all he observes that there are no cases of *Magia posthuma* (the term used before the introduction of the word vampirism in 1732) in towns where theologians or scientists live.

Other villages; to place him on a pyre – Schertz *considers* reasonable the choice of the inhabitants of Blov to consult with those of neighbouring villages. It always remained open to debate in such cases where to build a pyre and where to leave the ashes of the condemned; it is well known that the places of execution were often built outside the environs of the villages, such as at crossroads because these places did not belong to any village.

Blood poured out from him – In Schertz's time, many people still thought that a bleeding corpse was a secret sign of nature to indicate the culprit. For Schertz, this belief is at the origin of the rite of ordeal. Schertz, however, considers the ordeal as a "barbaric custom": Blood can pour out from a corpse from natural causes and not because of magic.

After the cremation, all the evil ceased – For Schertz, on the basis of study of ancient relevant legal literature, a lower court cannot judge a person who is dead. If we wish to consider a corpse as a criminal, we must collect a lot of evidence; otherwise we have no right to judge it. The crime has to be a real and proven offence.

Every night he rose - Referring to the theology and jurisprudence of his time and to the events narrated and "verified," Schertz has no problem stating that ghosts do exist.

When we speak of vampirism, we must therefore always refer to a dead person who somehow manages to rise from the other world and represents a danger to the community. The literature on vampirism, before and after Schertz, even if we do not include film and literary fiction, is today enormous. It is a belief that has spanned the history of mankind, probably from the upper Paleolithic until the period of industrialisation and electricity.

Vampirism, under whatever name, was also, for example, known in Mesopotamian cultures, especially those of the Akkadians and Assyrians, the written myths of which most likely reflected older Sumerian myths. For example, in the Akkadian version of the famous Sumerian myth 'Inanna's descent to the Netherworld', the goddess Ištar (Inanna for Sumerians) threatens: "I shall bring up the dead, they will devour the living" (West, 1997: 417).

It is also known that illnesses in Ancient Mesopotamia were attributed to the dead (see Scurlock, 2006), and the most dangerous of these dead, those who were buried improperly, were called *edimmu*. The Akkadian word *mītūti* is usually translated as the 'dead people' (see for example Abusch & Schwemer, 2010: 144, 329), yet Stephen Mitchell (2010: 136) does not hesitate to translate it with 'ghoul', which is the Arabic word for the harmful living dead.

Of course, in ancient Egypt, it was also extremely important to conduct funeral rituals without mistakes; otherwise the dead could come back and harm the living. But it is only in the later ancient Greece that we find a rich literature on the vampire, which was termed *empusa*. In Roman literature, Ovid called it *lemur*. A beautiful description of the *empusa*, which emphasizes his sexual hunger, is given to us by the Greek sophist Lucius Flavius Philostratus (2nd and 3rd Century CE) in his *Life of Apollonius of Tyana*. We also note that many translators into modern language, beginning from Frederick Cornwallis Conybeare, translated the ancient Greek *empusa* to the modern 'vampire' (see Conybeare, 1912: 407).

Furthermore, if we look at the classic novel known now as *Philinnion and Machates*, narrated by Phlegon of Tralles (2nd Century CE), and edited at the end of the 18th Century into modern language (see Hansen, 1996), we have no doubt that the vampiristic scheme was really well known in ancient Greece, long before the 18th-Century heyday of vampirism.

In Western barbaric and 'post-barbaric' Europe, we can find similar narrations as well. It is not, however, a case of literary transmission from the ancient world to medieval Northern Europe. The circumstance that the stories are in fact very similar is actually proof that the belief in vampires is much older than the Middle Ages and the ancient world. Among the Norsemen for example, as already pointed out long ago by the great Danish archaeologist Johannes Brøndsted (1890-1965), families knew that it was necessary to have an adequate reverence for death, otherwise they could become vampires. In these cases it was necessary to open the grave and "kill them again" (Brøndsted, 1960: 253).

For example, in *Laxdæla saga*, written in Iceland in the 13th Century, we are told that after Hrapp Sumarliðason's death in the year 950, he became a vampire, and it was only possible to destroy him ten years later thanks to the intervention of the noble Olaf. Olaf dug up the Hrapp's (undecayed) corpse, built a pyre, burnt him on it, and flung his ashes out to sea (see *Laxdæla saga*, chapters 17 and 19; see Press (ed.), 1899). In *Eyrbyggja saga* (see Magnússon & Morris (eds), 1992), written in the same period, we also learn of the transfer of corpses from grave to grave, i.e. a secondary burial. This was an ancient system of burial, preserved mainly in Eastern Europe (Maiello, 1996) and still practiced in the Balkans and Southern Italy. The secondary or double burial was a system that on the one hand allowed the community to ensure that the process of bodily decomposition had been brought to completion but on the other hand did not require such a waste of resources as did cremation. But in the case of very dangerous vampires, i.e. people who were already evil in their earthly life, there was no other way to definitively destroy a vampire than cremation. There are multifarious stories from across Europe which follow the same ideological pattern, despite taking place at different times. One of the best cases is provided by William of Newburgh (1136-1198) in his *History of English Affairs*, where he writes about the evil owner of Anantis Castle. This man wounded himself to death while he was watching the love games of his wife and a young lover. After the funeral, the evil man became a vampire and began to commit heinous murders.

Since it is a very good literary monument, the *History of English Affairs* is also considered a good source of ethnographic information, for example, that in the Middle Ages the only way to end the atrocities of a vampire was to cremate his corpse (see Stevenson, 1861: 660-661). William of Newburgh's report, together with other accounts from the Middle Ages, for example *The Enchanted Shoemaker of Constantinople* (see Summers, 1929: 93), reported by Walter Map (1135-1210) on a motif known also to Gervase of Tilbury (1150-1228), Roger of Hovedon (1174-1201), John Brompton (fl. 1436), and Sir John Mandeville (19th Century), became a basis for discussion for those European scholars who were concerned with witchcraft and posthumous magic.

However, in his legal analysis of vampirism, Carl Ferdinand Schertz takes another direction, analysing the writings of theoreticians of witchcraft, rather than the writings of narrators of ancient stories. Here is the bibliography of the Renaissance and Baroque authors he quotes. The following bibliography is still very important today for the study of vampirism, witchcraft, and the paranormal:

Matthias Wesenbeck, *Paratitla in Pandectarum iuris civilis libros quinquaginta*, Basel, Oporin, 1563;

James VI, King of Scotland, *Daemonologie, In Forme of a Dialogie, Divided into three Bookes*, Edinburg, Robert Walde-graue, 1597;

Prospero Farinacci, *Praxis et theoricae criminalis pars prima*, Venice, Varisco, 1589;

Giacomo Menochio, *De Præsumptionibus, conjecturis, signis, et indiciis, commentaria, In Sex distincta Libros*, Turin, Tarinus,1594;

Martin Antonio Del Rio, Disquisitionum magicarum libri sex, Louvain, Gerard Rivius, 1599-1600;

Giuseppe Mascardi, *Conclusiones omnium probationum, quae in vtroque foro quotidie versantur*, Turin, Tarinus, 1608;

Peter Thyraeus, *Demoniaci cum Locis infestis et Terriculamentis nocturnis: id est, libri tres*, Cologne, Cholinus, 1604;

Heinrich Kornmann, De miraculis mortuorum, Darmstadt, Wolff, 1610;

Alexander Trentacinque, *Practicarum resolutionum iuris libri tres*, Frankfurt am Main, Rulandiorum, 1610;

Jacques Gouthière, *De iure Manium, seu de Ritu, More et Legibus prisci Funeris, libri III*, Paris, Buon, 1615;

Christoph Besold, *Thesaurus practicus*, Tubinga, Brunnius, 1629;

Agostinho Barbosa, *Variae tractationes iuris*, Lyon, Laurenti Durand, 1631;

Johann Jacob Speidel, Notabilia iuridico-historico-politica, Strasbourg, Lazarius Zenzer, 1634;

Sigismund Finckelthaus, *Observationes practicae*, Leipzig, Gross, 1636;

Daniel Sennert, *Practicae medicinae libri 6*, Lyon, Ravaud, 1636;

Antonius Mattheaus, *De criminibus*, Utrecht, Waesberg, 1644;

Frierich von Spee – Hermann Schmidt, *Cautio criminalis seu de processibus contra sagas liber*, Frankfurt, Hummen, 1649;

Samuel Stryx, *Aisthetologia nomike sive Tractatus juridicus de jure sensum*, Frankfurt (Oder), 1665;

Justus Georg Schottelius, *De singularibus quibusdam et antiquis In Germania Iuribus et Observatis*, Frankfurt-Leipzig, Gottlieb Heinrich Grentz, 1671;

Bohuslav Balbín, Miscellanea Historica Regni Bohemiae III. Topographicus et chorographicus, Prague, Czernoch, *1681;*

Celestino Sfondrati, *Disputatio juridica de lege in praesumptione fundata*, Salzburg, Univ. Diss, 1681;

Justus Oldekop, *Observationes criminales practicae congestae,* Bremen, Justus & Jacob Köhler, 1685;

Joseph Bernard Glettle, *Jurispudentia terribilis*, Salzburg, Mayr, 1687;

August Benedict Carpzov, *De Transportatione Defunctorum Per Territorium Alienum*, Leipzig, Brandenburgerus, 1690;

Johann Heinrich Decker, *Spectrologia*, Hamburg, Liebernictel, 1690;

Christoph Kormart, *Tractatus iuridicus de jure consiliorum*, Dresden, Hübner, 1693;

Amandus Hermann, *Ethica sacra, scholastica, speculativo-practica; seu tractatus & disputationes morales de virtutibus*, Würzburg, Hertz, 1698;

Matthaeus Luls, *Dissertatio juridica inauguralis ad l*[egem] *IV. C*[odicis] *de sepulc.viol.,* Harderwijk, Sas, 1700;

Jan František Beckovský, *Poselkyně starých příběhův českých*, Prague, Jeřábek, 1700;

Tobias Grantz, *Defensio inquisitorum ex genuinis jurisprudentiae principis*, Frankfurt-Leipzig, 1702.

If we read the *Magia posthuma* carefully and take into account the bibliography used by Schertz, we must reject the stereotype of him as a 'dupe' and/or 'obscurantist'. The term "studied dupe" when referring to Schertz was, for example, used in 1986 by a high representative of the academic establishment of that time, in a book dedicated to witch-hunting in Europe (Šindelář, 1986: 215).

Schertz was adamantly against the exhumation and cremation of corpses suspected of vampirism because:

- *When handing down a judgment it is necessary to follow the law, not the precedents*
- *The 'old women' [i.e. the clairvoyants] have the right to be buried in consecrated earth*
- *We must not condemn anyone simply on the basis of superstition.*

Schertz realises that there are scientists and philosophers, such as Thomas Hobbes, who declare "Ghosts and sprites do not exist," but he believes in the possibility of the return of the dead for three reasons. The first is objective: At that time, it was impossible in Moravia and Silesia (i.e. the places where Carl Ferdinand Schertz lived and worked) to not believe in vampires since it was a totally widespread belief. The second was subjective: Schertz, in his own words, had direct experience with "*polter-geists*," as he called the dead disturbing the living. The third was that most scientists and philosophers of that time did not doubt the existence of ghosts. But for Schertz, the vampires were just the spirits of wandering souls, released in some way from purgatory. As a result, they just needed the appropriate prayers to find their peace.

With regards to the so-called *incubi*, who are rightfully often associated with vampires because of their sexual hunger and desire to drag their victims to the other world, Schertz considered these to be natural diseases rather than *demons*.

More importantly for Schertz, who was educated in jurisprudence, rather than in theology or philosophy, was the discussion on whether it was right to prosecute a corpse. Schertz recounts the few cases in which a regular tribunal decided to condemn a corpse, but these were very exceptional cases, such as those involving the crime of High Treason or "transvestism." The first case concerned so prominent a personality as that of Oliver

Cromwell, who was tried and condemned two years after his death: His corpse was dug up, hung in chains, and then beheaded. The second case concerned those "men who dress up as women, have sexual intercourse with men, and just after the examination of the corpse it becomes apparent that they had male genitalia." But Schertz argues that the majority of the cases of supposed *Magia posthuma* are just hasty exhumations, without a proper trial and therefore involving people who could not have accomplished great crimes.

The proof that Schertz understands the problems connected with vampirism in a rational manner lies in the fact that, for him, the dead are just dead, and condemnations can no longer harm them. Schertz notes that the real problem is actually with the families of the condemned. The families are not only subjected to public shame because of prejudice but are forced, due to the laws of the time, to pay all expenses related to the exhumation and cremation of the corpse. The families definitely pay for crimes that they and probably none of the dead ever committed.

All of these considerations lead us to affirm that:
-   *Carl Ferdinand Schertz was not a weirdo*
-   *The* Magia posthuma *exists and is not a mysterious lost book*
-   *Schertz's approach was in keeping with the science and theology of his time*
-   *If Schertz speaks without inhibition concerning vampires, it is because at that time it was absolutely impossible in Moravia and Silesia to not believe in vampires.*

Schertz's legal analysis of vampirism reflects a rational spirit, and his controversy with Hobbes from afar does not represent a denial of 17th-Century rationalism in the name of unproven obscurantism.

References

Abusch, T., & Schwemer, D. 2010. *Corpus of Mesopotamian Anti-witchcraft Rituals* (Vol. I.). Leiden: BRILL.

Brøndsted, J. 1960. *The Vikings*. Harmondsworth: Penguin.

Calmet, A. 1746. *Dissertations sur les apparitions des anges, des démons et des esprits, et sur les revenons et vampires de Hongrie, de Bohême, de Moravie et de Silésie*. Paris: de Bure l'aîné.

Calmet, A. 1850. *The Phantom World or, The philosophy of spirits, apparitions, &c, &c*. London: Richard Bentley.

Cary. 2009. *Vampire Lovers discussion*, 09 June. Retrieved 11 June 2014, from Goodreads: https://www.goodreads.com/topic/show/122947-vampire-books

Hansen, W. (ed.) 1996. *Phlegon of Tralles' Book of Marvels*. Exter: University of Exeter Press

Conybeare, F. (ed.) 1912. *Philostratus. The Life of Apollonius of Tyana. The Epistles of Apollonius and the tratise of Eusebius* (Vol. I.). London-New York: Macmillan.

Foster, P. 2002. *Blood Legacy*. Bloomington: iUniverse.

Introvigne, M. 1996. 'Satanism Scares and Vampires from the Eighteenth Century to the Contemporary Anti-Cult Movement', *Transylvanian Journal: Dracula and Vampire Studies 2/1*, pp. 31-45.

Jakobsson, Á. 2009. 'The Fearless Vampire Killers: A Note about the Icelandic Draugr and Demonic Contamination in Grettis Saga', *Folklore 120*, p. 307-316.

Keyworth, D.G. 2006. 'Was the Vampire of the Eighteenth Century a Unique Type of Undead-corpse?', *Folklore 117*, p. 241-260.

Lang, A. 1897. *A Book of Dreams and Ghosts*. London- New York-Bombay: Longmans, Green, & Co.

Magnússon, E., & Morris, W. (eds.) 1992. *Eyrbyggja saga*. London: Bernard Quaritch.

Maiello, G. 1996. 'Double Burial and Slav Specificity: Some Italian Considerations', *Acta Universitatis Carolinae. Philosophica et Historica* , 31-36.

Maiello, G. 2004. *Vampyrismus v kulturních dějinách Evropy*. Praha: NLN.

Maiello, G. 2014. *Vampyrismus a Magia posthuma*. Praha: Epocha.

Mitchell, S. 2010. *Gilgamesh. A New English Version*. New York: Simon and Schuster.

Niederle, L. 1916. *Život starých Slovanů* (Vol. II.1.). Praha: Bursík & Kohout.

Pedersen, N.K. 2009. 'Magia posthuma: a Weblog Approach to the History of Central and East European Vampire Cases of the 18th Century', *Kakanienrevisited* , 1-8.

Press, M.A.C. (ed.) 1899. *Laxdæla Saga*. London: J.M. Dent and co.

Schertz, C.F. 1704. *Magia posthuma*. Olomouc: Rosenburg.

Scurlock, J.A. 2006. *Magico-Medical Means of Treating Ghost-Induced Illness in Ancient Mesopotamia*. Leiden–Boston: Brill-Styx.

Šindelář, B. 1986. *Hon na čarodějnice. Západní a střední Evropa v 16.-17. století*. Praha: Svoboda.

Stevenson, J. (ed.) 1861. 'The History of William of Newburgh. The Chronicles of Robert de Monte'. In *The Church Historians of England* (Vol. IV. part II.). London: Seeley's.

Summers, M. 1929. *The Vampire in Europe*. London: London: Kegan Paul, Trench, Trubner and Co.

Vaillant, A. 1931. Slave commun *upiří*, s. cr. *vàmpīr. Slavia 10/4*, 673-679.

West, M.L. 1997. *The East Face of Helicon : West Asiatic Elements in Greek Poetry and Myth*. Oxford: Oxford University Press.

www.ingramcontent.com/pod-product-compliance
Lightning Source LLC
Chambersburg PA
CBHW021618270326
41931CB00008B/761